Collector's Guide to

Horsman Dolls

IDENTIFICATION & VALUES

1865–1950

Don Jensen

COLLECTOR BOOKS
A Division of Schroeder Publishing Co., Inc.

"America's best known and best loved dolls"

Cover design: Beth Summers
Book design: Holly C. Long

Front cover:
Left: 28" Sweetheart, dressed as Jeanette McDonald, 1938.
Center: 16" Dolly Rosebud, late 1920s.
Right: 24" Rosebud, 1940s.

Back cover:
11" Bright Star, late 1930s.

COLLECTOR BOOKS
P.O. Box 3009
Paducah, Kentucky 42002-3009
www.collectorbooks.com

Copyright © 2002 Don Jensen

The current values in this book should be used only as a guide. They are not intended to set prices, which vary from one section of the country to another. Auction prices as well as dealer prices vary greatly and are affected by condition as well as demand. Neither the author nor the publisher assumes responsibility for any losses that might be incurred as a result of consulting this guide.

Searching For A Publisher?

We are always looking for people knowledgeable within their fields. If you feel that there is a real need for a book on your collectible subject and have a large comprehensive collection, contact Collector Books.

Contents

Dedication

To Arlene, my literary advisor and in-house editor,
my "spell-checker," cheering section, doll buddy, best friend,
and, always, my love!

Acknowledgments

The list is long of those to whom I owe a debt of gratitude for their help and support in making this book possible.

At the head of the list must be Nancy Carlson, a great friend, wonderful loving soul, and acclaimed doll expert, who surely was my inspiration in tackling such a project, though, sadly, she did not live to see its publication.

Pat Schoonmaker, dear friend and mentor, showed me how to do doll research the "right way." Ursula Mertz has been a wonderful friend in so many ways, tangible and intangible, that I cannot fully acknowledge. This book would not exist without her help. Patsy Moyer offered advice, encouragement, and photographic support in equal measure, and for that I am sincerely grateful. The three are all well-known and accomplished authors, and if this book is but a fraction as successful as their own, I will be pleased, indeed.

John Arbeeny introduced me to Edward Horsman Jr., through the remarkable handwritten journals "Junior" wrote a century ago. John almost literally stumbled upon these two volumes more than 30 years ago, and I think it safe to say that they have impacted on his life in important ways. After our chance encounter on-line, he generously shared them and his insights into the younger Horsman's riveting personality.

Helen Fox Trowbridge, sculptress and Horsman's chief doll designer during the early years, was instrumental in its success, and by extension, in the development of the American doll industry. A long on-line search ultimately brought me to her sole surviving child, 80-year-old James Rutherford Trowbridge, and her granddaughter and namesake, Helen Hoffman.

Jim proved a wonderfully genial and helpful gentleman. And his niece, Helen, "keeper of the flame" for the Trowbridge family, graciously offered a wealth of information about her grandmother and her long under-appreciated artistic career.

In tracing the historical elements of the story, I received a lot of help. Internet resources were important, and via e-mail, I was assisted by many, but particularly Marie Kleman, James Hemenway Gibbs, and Linda Lau.

More traditional sources of information, including numerous libraries and archives, were mined for data with major help from Janet West (Port Washington, NY, Public Library), Ginny Potter (Cornwall, CT, Library), Helen V. Beckert (Free Public Library, Glen Ridge, NJ), Anita Schaeffer (Trenton Public Library, Trenton, NJ), Jennifer Moss (Richland County Public Library, Columbia, SC), Mrs. Philip W. Clark (archivist, Women's Club of Upper Montclair, NJ), Carol Sandler (Strong Museum, Rochester, NY), Penny Turley (House of Commons Information Office, London), Bruce Martin (Library of Congress), and professional genealogist Lance McRae.

This reference relies heavily on many people who said "yes" when I asked for help with photographs. Special thanks to those who have shared their doll pictures:

Cindy and Jim Adams, Bernice Allen, John Arbeeny, Juanita Austin, Gay Baron, Karen Barnum, Tracey Baumgartner, Cindy Blach, Dorothy Bohlin, Ann Boregino, Donna Boulanger, Myra Boyd, Rebecca Branscome, Danielle Brumit, Pat Buccolo, Diane Bucey, Marseille Bunk, Flo Burnside, Dee Cermak, Diane Chappell, Beverly Courtney, Debbie Crume, Kathy DeFinis, Diane Dustir, Leslie Falcon, Carol Ferguson, Kandy Ferriby, Julie Ghavam, Paula J. Giany, Willy Ginaven, Mary Evelyn Graf, Jean Grout, Betty Houghtaling, Gary Keller, Sue Kinkade, Stephanie Kornreich, Carol and Andrea Kowerdovich, Pat and Tom Lee, Mary Loy, Ruth MacDavitt, Joyce MacWilliamson, Katherine Manring, Frances Margulieux, Pamela Martinec, Deborah Miller, Bev Mitchell, Linda Mitchell, Donna Mullet, Chris Myer, Tammy Nall, Joan Nickel, Kathy Penn, Geri Perlstein, Barbara Pio, Patsy Prichard, Nancy Ringe, Jean Rollins, Joan Rollins, Karen Schell, Russ Sears, Nelda Shelton, Gay Smedes, Roy and Kathy Smith, Linda Sonntag, Shawn Stevens, Agnes Sura, Elizabeth Surber, Jeanne Swafford, Brenda Thomas, Sandra Tripp, Mary Whitney, Linda Woodhouse, Kandy Woods, and Valerie Zakzewski.

I am grateful for the photographic help offered by Sheri McMasters of McMasters Doll Auction, and Linda Edward of The Doll Museum, Newport, RI, as well as Celia's and Susan's Dolls and Collectibles, Children's Planet, Dollies in the Big Apple, Just Perfect Dolls and Antiques, and Sister Act Two.

And to everyone else who offered encouragement along the way, my sincere thanks!

Introduction

For years, Horsman's slogan claimed it was the "Best Known and Best Loved" name in American dolls. Arguably, it is true. For generations, hardly a little girl grew up without finding at least one Horsman doll under her Christmas tree. And virtually every collector today is familiar with the Horsman name, and many have wonderful examples of Horsman dolls in their collections.

But little has been known about the maker of these dolls, the E.I. Horsman Co., and its successors who used the trademarked name. And few are really aware of the countless types of Horsman dolls — with their cute faces, high quality construction, and attractive outfits — that have been sold for well over a century.

This is the first doll collector's book to tell the Horsman story. And a fascinating story it is too.

It is part history, an intriguing tale of an ambitious, successful entrepreneur and his initially reluctant, but ultimately enthusiastic and innovative son, who together played a critical role in the early development of American dolls. It is a story of other men, and women who followed in their footsteps, creating literally millions of well-made dolls that generations of ordinary American youngsters loved and cherished.

More importantly, it is the ultimate reference for collectors of Horsman dolls today, with descriptive listings and more than 400 illustrations. It includes color photographs of Horsman dolls, both commonly found and remarkably rare, plus many vintage catalog and advertising pictures, to help identify your dolls. Additionally, there is value information that will help you answer that important question: "How much is my doll worth?"

I hope that this book will be fascinating and fun and help you to better enjoy your collection of Horsman dolls!

About Doll Marks

To American doll makers, the identifying marks they molded into their composition dolls over the decades had great importance. These marks — the company name, its initials or, perhaps, a distinctive symbol on the back of the doll's head or neck — indicated to customers that they were getting the "real thing," not a cheap knock-off or copycat version of a popular doll.

But marking dolls had another, equally important reason. Like a wild animal marking its territory, companies used doll marks as a warning to would-be competitors in the jungle that was the American toy market: "This company will defend its copyrighted doll design. We will sue you!"

The importance of marking its dolls was a lesson E.I. Horsman Co. learned only belatedly, and, even then, imperfectly.

In the early years, Horsman often marked its dolls only with initials and the year of copyright, e.g., E.I.H. © 1910. But in 1926, the company lost a lawsuit against a competing firm it claimed had violated its copyright. After the judge ruled that initials alone provided inadequate identification to protect a copyright design, the firm became more careful about labeling dolls with the Horsman name.

But that did not always mean molding Horsman identification into the composition or, in later years, plastic dolls. Sometimes the name appeared only on paper labels or cardboard hangtags, usually discarded or lost soon after a child received her doll. This can cause identification problems for collectors today.

The oldest of the Horsman marks was its logo, a silhouette of the mythical centaur, half horse, half man, literally a "horse-man," which seems to date to about 1897. In early advertising, it is accompanied by the words, "Genuine Horsman 'Art' Doll." The centaur logo has appeared on Horsman labels, tags, ribbons, boxes, and advertising over the decades, but not impressed on composition or plastic dolls.

When Horsman did mark its doll heads, it did not do so in any standardized way. It used many different markings over the years. They include:

E.I.H (often with copyright symbol and the year, e.g. E.I.H. © 1910)

E.I.H. Co. or E.I.H. // Co.

E.I.H. Co. Inc.; E.I.H. © Inc.; or E.I.H. © Co. Inc.

EIH CO (in diamond)

E.I.H. © A.D.Co. (1919 – 1922, when Horsman and its chief doll supplier merged as E.I. Horsman and Aetna Doll Co.)

E.I. © H.C.; or E.I. © H. Co.; or E.I. © H. Co. Inc. (circa 1923 – 1926)

E.I. © H. Co. // E.I. Horsman // Inc. (after 1926)

E.I. HORSMAN CO. INC.

E.I. HORSMAN INC. // Made In // Germany

FULPER (vertically) // HORSMAN

HORSMAN // Nippon

HORSMAN

HORSMAN DOLL

Horsman Dolls, Inc.

HORSMAN DOLLS // Made in USA

HORSMAN // DOLL // MFG In USA

HORSMAN DOLL MFG. CO.

Made in USA // Horsman // Doll

A // HORSMAN // DOLL

This is not necessarily a complete list.

Other doll marks have been attributed to Horsman over the years, but the author has not been able to independently confirm that those so marked actually are Horsman dolls.

H © C (Perhaps indicating Horsman Co.; circa 1930s, 1940s)
H. C(I). Q. (With the smaller letter I within the C; possibly indicating Horsman Co. Inc. Quality. Quality dolls is a commonly used Horsman description; circa 1916)

About Doll Values

How much is my Horsman doll worth? That's a question with several possible answers.

On one level, the answer may be "priceless," that is, beyond monetary price. A doll from your own childhood, or your mother's or grandmother's, may have a value to you that cannot be measured in dollars! The same may be true of that certain doll you found in an antique shop or at a garage sale, which, for whatever reason, or no reason at all, just "speaks" to you.

But at a more practical level, most of us would like some sort of dollar value to put on a doll. We may want a clue to what price to charge for a doll we want to sell, or how much to pay for one we want to buy. We may wish to have a value for insurance purposes, or simply because we are curious about "how much is she worth."

Regardless of the reason, it is a near-universal question for doll collectors. It also is a question that should be approached cautiously. Unless it is a new, still-being-manufactured doll, we are talking about secondary market value, a dollar amount that is determined not by some manufacturer but by the interplay between specific buyers and specific sellers at specific times and places. Since those factors vary, there can be no one certain value for a doll. It will vary, depending....

Depending on what? On who is selling? On who is buying? On how badly they want to sell, or want to buy?

When is the transaction taking place? During the hectic shopping weeks before Christmas, or in late-January when everyone is strapped for cash? Where? At a posh antique boutique? A flea market? An annual high profile doll show? An eBay online auction? In New York or North Carolina or North Dakota?

How rare is the doll? Price, hence value, is determined by supply and demand. If the supply of a certain type of doll is small, either because few originally were manufactured or because few have survived the years, it may have a high value. But even a rare doll may have few collectors interested in buying it, and so it may not be highly valued after all.

What is the condition of the doll? Particularly with dolls made of composition and cloth, and to a lesser extent, plastics — materials used extensively in Horsman dolls over the decades — the passage of time has taken its toll. Perfect examples of vintage dolls are few. The better condition, the more complete, the closer to original condition, the more a doll is worth. Damaged and incomplete dolls, even if restored, are less in demand, hence less valuable than those in good condition that have never needed restoration.

Value — The Bottom Line

Doll values appear in the captions adjoining the photographs of dolls. No values are listed under the black and white illustrations reprinted from vintage catalogs and advertisements because these are not actual existing dolls for which today's value can be estimated.

Values may represent actual recent selling prices, owners' estimates of what their dolls are worth, or the author's estimate, based on experience, of what they might sell for today. Two similar dolls pictured might vary in value due to completeness and/or condition, or rarity of a particular outfit. Your doll's value might be more or less than those pictured, depending upon those same factors.

In short, consider the values in this book to be only a guide. Listed values should not be considered an offer to buy or sell a doll. The author and the publisher assume no responsibility for any loss or damage that might occur through the use of this book or the information it contains.

The Early Years

The story of Horsman dolls begins with Edward Imeson Horsman.

A seemingly simple beginning, but little about the Horsman family history is either as simple or straightforward as it may seem. For Edward Imeson Horsman was the name given to at least five generations of males in this fascinating and complex family.

The Horsman who in 1865 founded the firm that would become famous for its dolls was Edward I. Horsman Sr. His son was Edward I. Horsman Jr., who in his own right would become a bright but short-lived star in early twentieth century doll making. Junior's son, who died in infancy, was Edward I. Horsman III. And adding to the confusion, Horsman Sr.'s father and grandfather also were named Edward.

As surnames, both Imeson and Horsman have a long and proud history in Yorkshire, England, but for Horsman Sr., his particular ancestors were less illustrious than he might have wished.

Engraving of E.I. Horsman Sr. in his late 40s.

An up-by-the-bootstraps entrepreneur, he rose from a humble birth in Brooklyn, New York, on Nov. 25, 1843, to become a successful Manhattan merchant. Like many nineteenth century *nouveau riche*, he craved respect as much as the good life, but in New York society, bloodlines still meant more than money.

So, recent research shows, Horsman Sr. set out to improve his image, even if he had to alter history to do it, by adding a bit of nobility, and a hint of royalty, to his ancestry.

In about 1890, as president of E.I. Horsman Co., he sent a biographical sketch to the publisher of the *National Cyclopedia of American Biography*. That family history claimed his great-grandfather was Edward Horsman, a prominent Yorkshire gentleman. Further, it said, the next generation, a clergyman grandfather, William Horsman, was personal chaplain to the famed Duke of Wellington. William married the daughter of Sir John Dalrymple, 4th Baronet of Cousland, and sister of the 8th Earl of Stair, Sir John Hamilton Dalrymple of Oxenford Castle, Scotland.

Finally, Horsman Sr. claimed, William's son, Edward Horsman, his own father, was a Cambridge-educated barrister, who also married into nobility and through his wife had a link to the British royal house. This Edward, the biography noted, left the practice of law and entered English politics, serving successively as a Lord of the Treasury, Chief Secretary for Ireland, and finally, longtime and important Member of Parliament.

This was an impressive story, and, indeed, those prominent Horsmans do appear in the pages of British history. But in spite of the similarity in names, Edward I. Horsman Sr. was related to none of them. He'd simply grafted his branch onto a more illustrious family tree.

In fact, his Horsman ancestors, though also of sturdy Yorkshire stock, came to North America sometime in the late eighteenth century. His paternal grandfather, Edward Horsman, was born about 1775, and by 1800 was living in Boston. That same year, he married 20-year-old Elizabeth Oliver. They had at least four children, the oldest and his namesake being born in 1802.

Elizabeth died, probably in childbirth, in 1808, and the following year, Edward married his second wife, Mary Barnett. They would have at least five children during the following decade. He worked as a secretary or clerk to a prominent Bostonian but apparently fell on ill health and hard times. In 1819, though only 44, he died in the Boston poor house.

His son, Edward Horsman, grew up in Boston, but in the 1830s moved to Brooklyn, New York, where he worked as a printer. There are some hints that he may have worked for the *New York Herald*, a newspaper that coincidentally would hire his grandson as music critic nearly 60 years later.

In April 1839, Edward married British-born, 24-year-old Mary Pearson, some 13 years his junior. They would have at least three children, Ellen, born in 1842; Edward Imeson Horsman (later he would call himself E.I. Horsman Sr.), in 1843, and Emma, in 1849.

The son was a bright boy, though his education was limited to grammar school in Brooklyn. There is a story, told by Horsman himself many years later, that he got his entrepreneurial start at 14, manufacturing and selling baseballs after school.

In 1859, at the age of 16, he went to work as a $2-a-week errand boy for Paton & Co., a New York import house at 341 Broadway. He worked there for a half-dozen years, learning the basics of business. Though of an age when many young Americans saw combat, as far as is known, he did not serve in the Civil War.

Ambitious and energetic, he set out in business on his own in 1865, at the age of 22, making and selling "games and home amusements" in a shop at 105 Maiden Lane in New York.

About that time he met Florence Lewis Benton, the Virginia-born daughter of Brooklyn merchant Thomas Godwin Benton and Eliza Pitts Flynn Benton. On April 22, 1869, they were married at Holy Trinity Church in Brooklyn.

At first they lived at 92 Second Place, but later moved to 143 Berkley Street, also in Brooklyn. They would have five children, four of whom would survive to adulthood. They included a son, Edward I. Horsman Jr., born March 16, 1873, and three daughters, Florence, Mary, and Eliza Horsman. The fifth child apparently died at birth.

Also in 1869, the 26-year-old entrepreneur moved his business to 100 William Street, where he occupied the storefront and the basement. In the next decade, he expanded into adjoining stores and then into the original "Flatiron Building" in downtown Manhattan.

Sporting goods formed an important part of Horsman's business, and he managed to catch each new craze as it came along. His earliest success in the late 1860s came with croquet sets. Archery became popular in the late 1870s, and he employed a hundred workers making bows and arrows.

Lawn tennis gained popularity starting in the 1880s, and Horsman-made tennis racquets sold in large numbers. Horsman himself became a devoted tennis enthusiast and would still be playing at the age of 72.

In the 1870s, E.I. Horsman Sr. began traveling regularly to Europe to import "toys, fancy goods and novelties." He was a regular visitor to Nuremberg, the German toy making "capital" and to the doll factories in Thuringia. And although he would sometimes claim to be descended from a line of German toy makers, this was as fanciful as his noble ancestry.

By the mid-1870s, Horsman's company was selling dolls — bisque-head imports from Germany — beginning a tradition that has continued for a century and a quarter.

Horsman's wholesale business expanded, and his 1885 catalog included a wide variety of imported dolls in many sizes. Listed were white dolls, black dolls, dressed and undressed, with bodies of kid leather, cloth or papier-maché; German and French bisque head dolls, some with human hair wigs; dolls made of an early type of composition, cloth rag dolls, wax dolls. There were tiny china dolls that wholesaled at only 6 cents a dozen, and large, gorgeously dressed French bisque types with a wholesale price of more than $20 each, a remarkably expensive doll considering that one could buy a fancy, 14-karat gold pocket watch for less than half that price.

In the nineteenth century, E.I. Horsman Co. was known more for its games and sports equipment than for dolls. Early lawn tennis rackets like this Horsman set from the early 1880s came in colorfully illustrated wooden boxes. Horsman Sr. was an early tennis enthusiast and played the game for many years.

An expanding New York wholesale district was moving slowly uptown, and in May 1891, the E.I. Horsman Co. followed. Surely there was some nostalgic pleasure when the company moved to 341 Broadway, the former home of the Paton and Co. import house where Horsman had begun his mercantile career 32 years earlier.

But only four months later, on Aug. 23, that venerable building burned down. Horsman reopened for business in a nearby vacant store the next day. By December, the fire-destroyed building had been rebuilt.

Whether the "polishing" of his ancestry had helped or not, by the 1890s, the 50-year-old Horsman Sr. was an important and respected New York merchant. He cut an impressive figure, a stocky five feet, nine inches tall, 200 pounds, with steel gray hair and dark blue eyes. Befitting his newfound social status, he was senior warden of Brooklyn's St. John's Episcopal Church; a charter member of the Museum of Arts and Sciences; a member of the Brooklyn Institute, the Montauk Club, and the Brooklyn Riding and Driving Club.

Horsman's wholesale catalog from 1892.

Indestructible Dolls.

10-I	0 75	50-I	4 00
15 I	1 25	75 I	6 00
20-I	1 50	90-I	8 00
25-I	2 00	100-I	9 00
35-I	2 50	150-I	12 00

Model Rag Dolls.

75-MR	6 00	150-MR	12 00
90-MR	8 00	200-MR	15 00
100-MR	9 00	250-MR	18 00

Fine French Bisque Dolls.

150-F	12 00	500-F	36 00
200-F	15 00	600-F	48 00
250-F	18 00	750-F	60 00
300-F	24 00	1000-F	78 00
400-F	30 00	1200-F	96 00

Fine French Bisque Dressed Dolls.

500-FF	36 00	1500-FF	120 00
600-FF	48 00	2000-FF	160 00
750-FF	60 00	2500 FF	200 00
1000-FF	78 00	3500-FF	250 00
1200-FF	96 00		

Bisque Dolls with Worsted Dresses.

100-BD	9 00	250-BD	18 00
150-BD	12 00	300-BD	24 00
200-BD	15 00		

Dressed Wax Dolls

25-DW	2 00	100-DW	9 00
50-DW	4 00	150-DW	12 00
75-DW	6 00	200-DW	15 00
90-DW	8 00	250-DW	18 00

China Limb Dolls.

No.	per gross.	No.	per gross.
5-CL	3 75	12-CL	9 00
7-CL	5 00	15-CL	10 00
10-CL	7 50		
No.	per doz.	No.	per doz.
18-CL	1 00	50-CL	3 00
20-CL	1 50	60-CL	3 50
25-CL	1 75	75-CL	5 00
30-CL	2 00	90 CL	6 00
35-CL	2 25	100-CL	8 00

China Babies. (White.)

No.	per gross.	No.	per gross
1	$ 75	5	3 75
2	1 25	10	6 00
3	2 00	15	9 00

Black China Babies.

Same assortment and prices as white.

Dolls Heads.

No.	per gross.	No.	per gross
5 China Heads	3 75	25 China Heads	16 50
10 " "	7 50	35 " "	18 00
15 " "	10 50	50 " "	24 00
20 " "	13 50		

Patent Heads Without Hair.

	per doz.		per doz.
10	75	35	1 75
15	1 00	50	2 00
20	1 25	75	2 50
25	1 50	100	3 00

Patent Heads With Hair.

	per doz.		per doz.
25	1 75	60	3 75
30	2 00	75	4 50
35	2 25	90	5 25
40	2 50	100	6 00
50	3 00		

Model Wax Heads.

	per doz.		per doz.
75	6 00	250	15 00
90	7 00	300	18 00
100	8 00	350	21 00
125	9 00	400	24 00
150	10 50	450	30 00
200	12 00	500	36 00

Model Wax Heads.
(SLEEPING EYES,)

	per doz.		per doz.
100	8 00	300	18 00
125	9 00	350	24 00
150	10 50	400	36 00
200	12 00	500	42 00
250	15 00	600	48 00

Model Washable Heads.
WITH HAIR.

	per doz.		per doz.
50	4 00	90	6 00
60	4 50	100	7 50
75	5 00	125	9 00

Bisque Heads.
WITH WHITE FUR HAIR.

	per doz.		per doz.
50	4 00	125	9 00
60	4 50	150	10 50
75	5 00	175	12 00
90	6 00	200	15 00
100	7 50		

Fine French Bisque Heads.
WITH NATURAL HAIR.

	per doz. net.		per doz. net.
150	10 50	350	24 00
175	12 00	400	30 00
200	15 00	450	36 00
250	18 00	500	42 00
300	21 00	600	48 00

Kid Doll Bodies.

	per doz.		per doz.
1	2 75	5	5 00
2	3 00	6	6 00
3	3 75	7	7 50
4	4 50	8	9 00

Kid Bodies with Bisque Arms.

	per doz.		per doz.
1	4 25	5	7 50
2	5 00	6	9 00
3	5 50	7	12 00
4	6 50	8	14 75

Fine Kid Bodies with Stockings and Shoes.

	per doz.		per doz.
1	7 00	5	12 00
2	8 00	6	13 50
3	9 00	7	16 00
4	10 00	8	18 00

Jewelry, Hats, Shoes, Stockings and Toilet Sets of all Kinds.

Doll page from a nineteenth century E.I. Horsman Co. wholesale catalog.

The list of guests at the 1895 wedding of his daughter, Florence, also attests to his prominence. Attending were Garret A. Hobart, who would be elected U.S. Vice President in the next year's election, and Thomas F. Bayard Sr., Ambassador to Great Britain and former Secretary of State. Other guests included the Rev. Lyman Abbott, theologian and author, the "Billy Graham" of his day; Judge William Jay Gaynor, Justice of the New York Supreme Court and soon-to-be New York mayor; famed international scholar and historian William Elliot Griffis; ex-congressman and Brooklyn's mayor, David A. Boody; LeBaron Bradford Prince, former New York legislator and most recently, governor of New Mexico Territory, and Dr. D.B. St. John Roosa, prominent surgeon and president of the New York Academy of Medicine.

In May 1891, E.I. Horsman Co. moved to 341 Broadway, but several months later, the building was badly damaged by fire. On Dec. 1, the firm reopened the retail showroom in its reconstructed building.

Imported German bisque head dolls shown in 1891 Horsman advertising.

Though generally thought of today as a doll maker, the E.I. Horsman Co. of the late nineteenth and early twentieth centuries primarily was not a manufacturer. While the company did some manufacturing and assembly work, and in the 1890s maintained a "manufactory" at Valley Falls, near Providence, Rhode Island, Horsman Sr. usually described himself as a merchant.

But his company was more complex. Initially, it had some retail trade, but mostly it was a distributor and a manufacturers' agent, with a rather extensive wholesale catalog of toys, games, sporting goods and novelties, sold to outlets, large and small, throughout the U.S.

An advertising illustration from the 1890s shows imported dolls on display in the E.I. Horsman Co. retail salesroom in New York City.

1897 engraving of Horsman's building at 512 Broadway.

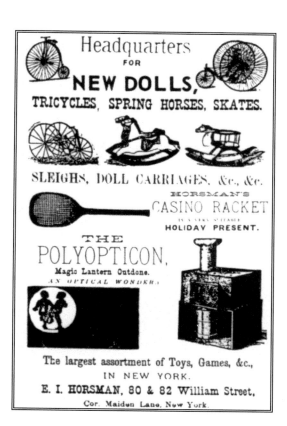

Horsman's Christmas catalog from 1886.

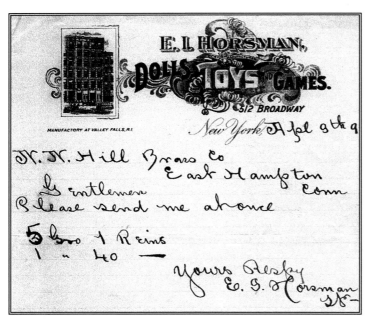

Business correspondence from 1897, written and signed by E.I. Horsman Sr.

The Horsman company also was a toy importer, and, from its earliest days, an assembler of dolls from imported parts, particularly German-made bisque heads.

Some have described the company as an American version of a "verleger," a German term for a seller who initiates and designs a doll or toy, retains all patents and trademarks, but owns no factories or production facilities.

A "verleger" contracted with factories to produce the playthings that it then sold exclusively. A 1914 Horsman catalog said, "We speak invariably as either the producers or first-hand distributors of the goods enumerated."

The definition of "verleger" would accurately describe the arrangement Horsman had with the Aetna Doll and Toy Co., the manufacturer that made Horsman's Can't Break 'Em composition dolls beginning in 1909. It wasn't until 1919, when both companies merged to form what for several years was called the E.I. Horsman and Aetna Doll Co., that it could really be considered a doll manufacturer.

Horsman showrooms at 380 – 382 Broadway in 1901.

Employees of the Aetna Doll and Toy Co. "cook" kettles of the secret mixture known as Can't Break 'Em composition.

Molding department of the Aetna Doll and Toy Co., maker of composition dolls for E.I. Horsman Co.

After being painted, the finished heads for the Can't Break 'Em composition dolls were dried on racks.

In the business community, Horsman Sr. was a member of the New York Chamber of Commerce, and as a member of a special "Committee of 100" prominent New Yorkers, he was a leader in the campaign to locate the World's Fair of 1892 – 1893 in New York City. He lobbied the nation's lawmakers, spoke before the U.S. Senate on behalf of New York's bid, and was in Washington when the disappointing vote was taken in the House of Representatives that gave the Columbian Exposition to rival Chicago.

Nonetheless, when that World's Fair opened, the E.I. Horsman Co. was in Chicago displaying its line of toys. Until 1919, when the company dropped its other lines to concentrate exclusively on making dolls, its catalogs included a wide range of playthings.

Popular crazes in which the E.I. Horsman Co. either led or played a role included jigsaw puzzles, in the early 1900s. Horsman's puzzles — called Perplexyu at first, but soon changed to Confusyu because of a confusing similarity with the name of a competitor's puzzles — were a smash hit among the social elite.

A 1914 catalog was filled with non-doll items, from Ouija boards to the Symmetroscope, an improved kaleidoscope with revolving lenses and mirrors; from a battery operated Electric Questioner, a quiz game, to a "scientific" mechanical baseball game endorsed with the signatures of Ty Cobb and Christy Mathewson. Construction toys included Bill Deezy, a predecessor of Erector; Richter's Anchor Blocks and Peg Lock, a Lego-like building set. There were toy telephones, telegraphs, and typewriters, lead soldiers, cap pistols and holsters, Daisy air rifles, and, a Horsman specialty, a series of elaborate kites.

Box kites were among the popular "scientific" novelties sold by E.I. Horsman Co. in the 1890s.

Horsman's picture jigsaw puzzles were all the rage in the early 1900s.

During the first decade of the twentieth century, E.I. Horsman Co. was headquartered at 367 Broadway in New York City.

Horsman Becomes a Brand

In the early 1890s, most dolls the company sold were imported and if marked at all, still carried the name of the manufacturer, such as Kestner and Jumeau. The beginning of the Horsman Dolls brand identity probably dates to 1897, when the company adopted a banner type label identifying Horsman Art Dolls, and including its logo, an outline of a centaur, part horse, part man.

The company registered its first solid success when it introduced a series of cloth dolls in its 1893 wholesale catalog. It called them Baby Land, but later would modify the name to Babyland Rag dolls. It was a name that would continue in the product line — though the dolls changed considerably — until the mid-1920s.

Over the years, Babyland Rag cloth dolls were made in many sizes, up to 30 inches, with hand painted features and, from 1907, also with photographically realistic "Life Like" lithographed faces. Some Babyland Rag types had mask-like molded fabric faces and for many years were made exclusively for Horsman by a Jersey City, New Jersey, manufacturer, Albert Bruckner.

A small illustrated Horsman brochure from 1912 included the last 12 lines of the following poem, describing the attractions of the Babyland Rag line that appeared in the catalog.

A MESSAGE FROM BABYLAND
Come big and come little, to Babyland come,
And see each sweet Babyland pet;
There are Topsy and Fancy, good Dinah and Jack,
And Baby, the sweetest one yet.
I can't stop to name them, but take a good look
At each pretty dolly you'll find in this book;
They have beautiful dresses, so pretty and bright,
Made of daintiest ginghams, the "newest thing" — quite —
And other crisp fabrics, pink, blue, red and white,
The quaint little bonnet, with ruffle of lace,
Adds style to the costume, and sets off the face.
Their bodies with cotton are all firmly filled,
And they're made after patterns of very best build.
And though you should squeeze them, or throw them about,
They never are broken, no sawdust comes out,
With neat shoes and stockings, their small feet are clad;
If their faces get dirty, it isn't so bad,
For soap and clean water will make them all right,
Not hurting the colors, but leaving them bright.
Then when the evening brings quiet and rest,
The dolls — like the children — can all be undressed;
In fact there's no doll, be it ever so grand,
That is better for children, than our Babyland.

As the twentieth century dawned, times were good, and President William McKinley was re-elected to a second presidential term on his promise of a continued "Full Dinner Pail" for the American workingman. But for the Horsman company, things turned inexplicably sour.

E.I. Horsman Sr.

"Edward I. Horsman Fails," read the small headline on a two-paragraph brief in the Jan. 3, 1901, issue of the *New York Times*. "Broadway Dealer in Toys Files Petition in Bankruptcy."

It quoted Alfred W. Bowie, temporary receiver of the assets and the Horsman company's treasurer, as saying "last evening it was found that Mr. Horsman owed more than he could pay, and it was deemed best for the interests of all concerned that he go into bankruptcy." Horsman had liabilities of $180,000 and assets of $172,000, Bowie said.

No reason for the financial problems was given. Bowie told the newspaper only that "Business had gone behind lately."

The rest of the story is told in a series of entries in the diary of 27-year-old Edward Horsman Jr., who though still remarkably disinterested in the family business, was very concerned about his father:

"January 28, 1901: Home at 6, dressed and had dinner. Father arrived with the supreme good news of the concurrence of his creditors in his settlement on the basis of 50 percent. I am more thankful than words will tell, and he is infinitely relieved.

"Feb. 11: Good news from the Pater when he arrived in the matter of his second creditors meeting today. No obstacles now stand in the way to a discharge from bankruptcy 10 days hence.

"Feb. 23: Returning home found Father in good spirits from his Western jaunt. It rejoices me that today his affairs were finally adjudicated by the court and he was discharged from his bankruptcy."

Horsman Sr. had learned an important lesson, though. Later that year, he incorporated the Horsman company. Any future financial problems his business might suffer would not again threaten him with personal bankruptcy. The financial clouds had passed, and he never looked back.

But he was looking to the future, a future he had long hoped would see his only son active in the family business. Technically, Edward Jr. was vice president of the firm, for he was so listed in the 1901 incorporation, but it was mostly a "paper title." As the trade magazine *Playthings* later put, young Horsman took "little or no stock of the great romance of business as such."

Edward Horsman Jr. was born in Brooklyn on March 16, 1873. As the only son in an increasingly affluent, upwardly mobile merchant family, he attended private schools. At Cathedral School of St. Paul in Garden City, Long Island, he was a prize essayist and senior captain of the military school's Cadet Corps. He graduated in June 1890.

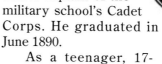

E.I. Horsman Jr.

As a teenager, 17-year-old Edward was caught up in the tiddlywinks — then called tiddledy-winks — game craze that swept the U.S. in 1890. He devised a version that combined tiddlywinks and tabletop tennis. His father patented the game and rules for "Parlor Tennis" in young Edward's name. It proved to be a moneymaker.

"E.I. Horsman (Sr.) ... is wearing a 7x9 smile these days," said the trade publication, *The American Stationer* in its Oct. 9, 1890 issue. "He has set the whole world by the ears with his (game) and dealers are fairly tumbling over each other in their haste to get orders in early...however to keep up, he has adopted the plan of sending a dozen to dealers who order a gross."

In a follow-up article, the magazine quoted Horsman Sr. as saying, "See that bundle of letters...every one of them orders for my favorite game, and they've got to be answered before I go to my dinner. Tiddledy Winks...is a great thing, I tell you, but I cannot stop to explain why just now. Come again after the holidays when the rush is over, and we will confer together on the subject!"

The company followed up early in 1891 with another game, a combination of quoits and tiddlywinks called Ring-a-Peg, which perhaps also was invented by Edward Jr., though that can't be definitely established through patent records.

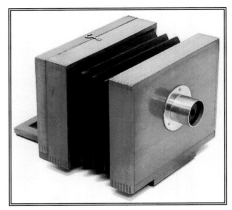

Edward Horsman Jr., a dedicated amateur photographer throughout his life, may have learned his skills with the No. 3 Eclipse, a brass-trimmed cherry wood camera with folding bellows sold by his father's company in the 1890s.

Edward became a skilled photographer, perhaps using one of the Horsman No. 3 Eclipse cameras his father's company sold. In later years, a *Who's Who* biographical entry would report Edward's interest in "color photography," which in those pre-WWI days must have meant hand-tinting black-and-white photos. He also loved traveling and touring the eastern seaboard by motorcar.

Edward's real interest, though, was music. In the early 1890s, he studied composition and choral direction, both in the U.S. and in Europe. He also became an accomplished organist. In 1898, he became organist and choir-master at St. Ann's Church. In 1902 he moved to a similar position at St. Luke's Episcopal Church, and from 1904 to 1906, served St. Andrew's Episcopal Church.

As a composer, he first gained attention in the music world with organ and choral compositions, including anthems, church services, and recital pieces. After about 1912, young Horsman began composing what then were known as "ultra modern songs." Some became popular in their day, including "The Bird of the Wilderness," which received a merit award for American songs and was performed by well-known concert soprano, Alma Gluck. In 1917, he directed his own patriotic choral work, "Stand Up, Stand Up, America" at Carnegie Hall.

Edward took on a part-time job as music and drama critic for the *New York Herald* in 1901, a post he held for five years until the demands of his developing business career grew too great.

Thanks to boyhood chum and lifelong friend, artist Vaughan Trowbridge, Edward's knowledge and appreciation of art were substantial as well. For some years, he made summer visits to Trowbridge's Paris studio, and often the two traveled around Europe together. Also, Edward sponsored New York art exhibits of works by his friend as well as those of other promising young artists.

He had an eye for beauty, says John Arbeeny, who has come to know Horsman Jr. through several remarkable journals the young man kept during his travels abroad in 1898 and 1901. Beauty revealed itself to Edward in the worlds of art, music, and poetry, in the blending voices of his youth choir, in a woman's personality, in the architecture of a centuries-old French church, in a dramatic line delivered by Sarah Bernhardt, in willows weeping over the banks of the Thames. Horsman was, as many would note, unique!

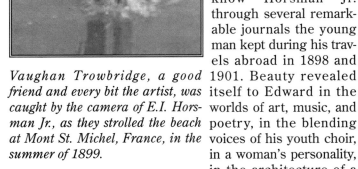

Vaughan Trowbridge, a good friend and every bit the artist, was caught by the camera of E.I. Horsman Jr., as they strolled the beach at Mont St. Michel, France, in the summer of 1899.

E.I. Horsman Jr. is shown composing music at the organ in about 1917.

Among his many interests, however, business was not initially included, although he did undertake a few special assignments for his father while traveling in England.

The first was a disaster. In the summer of 1899, Edward called upon Dean & Son, Ltd., a prominent Lon-

Edward I. Horsman Jr. works at his desk in rented quarters during his visit to London in the summer of 1899.

don publishing firm, to collect on an overdue account. The British firm had bought Horsman merchandise — probably including Babyland Rag dolls — on consignment and owed a substantial amount of money. In dealing with its representative, a fellow named Green, the somewhat naïve 25-year-old was overmatched.

"I have to charge against Green something more than the possession of a repellant personality," Edward wrote in his journal, "namely — I hate to use the words — sharp practice."

Not only did Green cheat E.I. Horsman Co., his cavalier attitude toward the young American was an insult. "I'm at a loss to know whether to feel most angry or most humiliated," Edward wrote. "Faugh! It disgusts me and angers me to write about him. Angers me too that I should not have been able to find the words to tell him what I thought of him!"

The incident seems to have led to a break in relations between the two companies — though some years later they would be restored to the benefit of both. It also may have led to the London firm forming a subsidiary that, in time, would manufacture its own cloth dolls. That subsidiary would be called Dean's Rag Book Co. Ltd.

More pleasant were Edward's dealings with another customer, Arthur Pain Co., a pyrotechnic firm on Walworth Road in London. Pain provided fireworks for public celebrations, regattas, and parades for British troops returning home from South Africa. These events also included the flying of large, colorful kites, which Pain ordered from Horsman.

Edward tried to interest Pain in a new idea he had for suspending advertising from these oversized kites. The proposal was well received, but such "sky signs" were found to be illegal under British law. Horsman did not abandon the idea, however, and in 1908 the company made headlines in New York City by flying a pair of box kites over lower Broadway trailing a 36-foot banner promoting "Free Advertising in the Sky — E.I. Horsman Co."

When E.I. Horsman Jr. turned 30 in 1903, however, he seemingly took stock of his life's direction and decided it was time to change course.

He married his longtime "fair lady," Ethel Hull Herrick, daughter of the former vice president of Thomas Edison's General Electric Co. Following her faith, he left the Episcopal Church and became a Christian Scientist. And he became the father of a son, Edward I. Horsman III, a fifth generation to bear the name.

Horsman made headlines by flying kits training a banner promoting "Free Advertising in the Sky."

Ethel Hull Herrick in London in 1901. Two years later, she would become Mrs. Edward I. Horsman Jr.

About the same time, his interest in the family company also took a 180-degree turn. "In the old days," *Playthings* noted, "Junior was a musical reporter and critic, a duty that caused his father no little worry for fear that the son would become utterly spoiled for business."

Now, though, things changed, and it was not just a "battlefield conversion" to business either. Though Horsman Jr. — still Edward to his artistic friends but Junior to his new business associates — never abandoned his early interests, continuing to compose music and champion the causes of young artists, he threw himself wholeheartedly into his work. He brought a finely tuned appreciation for artistic design, a quality his father never had, to the family firm.

Playthings called him a man of wide activities in thought as well as in deed, and noted his "artistic equipment was a great aid to him in his work."

Largely because of his efforts, the E.I. Horsman Co. would produce some remarkable new dolls during the next decade and a half, its "golden era." Soon the company would be one of the most important U.S. doll makers and a recognized leader in the rapidly developing American toy industry.

As *Playthings* advised in a 1917 "snapshot" of the transformed Junior: "Do not be too hasty in classifying a man — for you can never tell!"

Young Horsman virtually took over the company's doll business, and soon it was booming. The basic ingredient that allowed him to work such important changes was a soupy mixture — 67 percent glue and 11 percent each of glycerin, white zinc oxide, and Japanese wax — that was called Can't Break 'Em composition. It was a story that had begun some years earlier.

At that time, Germany and its toy making industry had a virtual monopoly of the doll market. No other country, and surely not the United States, the largest importer of dolls, seemed able to compete. But German bisque dolls, however popular in the nineteenth century, had a fatal flaw. They were easily broken in play. So would-be competitors began turning their attention to making unbreakable heads that could compete with the fragile bisque dolls.

There were many attempts, with varying degrees of success, but a major breakthrough in producing an unbreakable composition material was made in Russia in the early 1880s. Solomon D. Hoffmann brought the secret to the U.S. in 1892. He had obtained a patent for his process in Russia, and, on April 23, 1892, filed for a U.S. patent for making heads and limbs of dolls. The patent — No. 480,094 — was granted on Aug. 2. *Playthings*, in 1912, claimed that it was Hoffmann who coined the term, Can't Break 'Em.

This very rare 18" Can't Break 'Em composition doll made by Solomon D. Hoffmann was discovered recently by the author. The shoulder plate is stamped Absolutely Unbreakable/ /Patented Aug. 2nd 1892, and is incised F.A.D.F., for First American Doll Factory. This "Mother of American Composition Dolls" looks similar to German "patent washable" papier-mache head types from the same 1892 – 1895 period. $250.00.

Hoffmann started a small factory in Brooklyn, calling it, not quite accurately, the First American Doll Factory. The dolls he made were described as "exceedingly light, practical, indestructible," everything that bisque porcelain dolls were not.

The composition was poured into plaster molds at about room temperature. As it began to solidify, the still-liquid center was poured off, and the layer adhering to the mold was allowed to dry. The heads and limbs then were sanded smooth, dipped in a similar flesh-tinted composition, and dried. Facial features were hand painted, and the doll parts then were dipped in a clear collodion bath to protect and seal the surface.

Except for their composition heads, his dolls presumably looked a great deal like their imported German competitors. The business continued in a small way for several years.

Hoffmann, 54, died of tuberculosis on July 10, 1897, in New York City. His widow, and later his son, carried on. The composition formula was a closely held secret. A family member personally mixed each batch in a closed room. In 1909, the

Benjamin Goldenberg, president of the Aetna Doll and Toy Co., exclusive supplier of Can't Break 'Em composition dolls to the E.I. Horsman Co.

company's assets were sold to Benjamin Goldenberg of the Aetna Toy Animal Co. The business he acquired consisted of a few workers, three sewing machines, and a large loft, which, it was said, contained not much more than sunshine and good ideas. But Goldenberg brought a new dynamic to doll making. He moved into a larger factory at 28-30 Waverly Place, and renamed his company the Aetna Doll and Toy Co.

Soon, the huge New York distributor, George Borgfeldt & Co. was advertising Aetna's line of "Can't Break 'Em dolls, larger in size, better quality," made in "a modern factory, well equipped with up-to-date machinery operated by competent and expert toy makers."

"Can't Break 'Em" DOLLS

LARGER IN SIZE

BETTER QUALITY

RETAIL AT POPULAR PRICES

Can't Break 'Em Dolls are now made by the **AETNA DOLL AND TOY CO.**, celebrated for their famous **AETNA LINE OF TOY ANIMALS, PLAY SUITS, ETC.**

Already well known by the trade, Can't Break 'Em Dolls will now be better than ever. All the good features possessed by the Dolls will be retained, while improvements in construction and workmanship will be made.

A modern factory, well equipped with up-to-date machinery operated by competent and expert toy makers, insures for Can't Break 'Em Dolls better quality and bigger value.

Dealers should not fail to see this unique Doll, the only one of its kind, absolutely unbreakable, manufactured in the United States.

Can't Break 'Em Dolls are one of the many lines handled exclusively by us and not to be seen elsewhere.

WRITE FOR SAMPLES AND PRICES.

GEO. BORGFELDT & CO.

48-50 West 4th Street   NEW YORK

In this 1909 Playthings advertisement, wholesaler George Borgfeldt & Co. announced that it was the exclusive distributor of Aetna's Can't Break 'Em dolls. Soon after, however, Horsman turned the tables on its large competitor, contracting with Aetna to "control" its entire production of the unbreakable dolls.

PLAYTHINGS

Important to Importers of Dolls!

"Can't Break 'Em" Dolls

Manufactured by the

Aetna Doll and Toy Company

E. I. HORSMAN CO.

are pleased to announce that they have secured **Exclusive Control** of the manufacture and distribution of this celebrated line.

The entire line has been reconstructed in such a way as to establish doll making in America on a substantial basis

New and beautiful designs made of the "Can't Break 'Em" material will be on display in our sample rooms on Jan. 3d

No Buyer should place his import doll order till he has seen the NEW and STARTLING lines we have to offer.

Manufacturers' Agents

E. I. HORSMAN CO.   365 Broadway
NEW YORK

Kindly Mention PLAYTHINGS When Writing to Advertisers.

Horsman announced a special sales agreement with Aetna Doll and Toy Co., manufacturer of its Can't Break 'Em composition dolls.

We are Sole Selling Agents for the Famous

"Can't Break 'Em" Dolls

MANUFACTURED BY THE

Aetna Doll and Toy Company

The entire line has been reconstructed in such a way as to establish doll making in America on a substantial basis.

New and beautiful designs now on display in our sample rooms. Send for price list.

MANUFACTURERS' AGENTS

E. I. HORSMAN COMPANY, 365 Broadway
NEW YORK

Can't Break 'Em dolls, Borgfeldt announced, are "handled exclusively by us and not to be seen elsewhere."

Borgfeldt was a major competitor of E.I. Horsman Co., and the Horsmans, father and son, were not to be outdone. Clearly they offered Goldenberg a deal he could not refuse. Not long after Borgfeldt's advertisement appeared in *Playthings*, another ran in the trade magazine. "Important to importers of Dolls! Can't Break 'Em Dolls, manufactured by the Aetna Doll and Toy Company. E.I. Horsman Co. are pleased to announce that they have secured Exclusive Control of the manufacture and distribution of this celebrated line!"

The Horsmans had won a major victory, exclusive control of everything Aetna produced. The first smash hit was Billiken, a composition head, plush-bodied novelty, the first copyrighted doll sponsored by Horsman. They sold 200,000 Billikens in the first six months of production.

Earlier, Horsman and Borgfeldt had gone head to head in marketing Teddy Bears — it was, in fact, a Horsman ad in September 1906 that had given the name Teddy's Bears to the already popular stuffed toy — and now there was a race to see which could capture what appeared to be a real market for unbreakable composition dolls.

The company followed Billiken's success with a more traditional doll, Baby Bumps, a knockoff of a German import, a Kammer & Reinhardt character face, which proved to be a big seller for Horsman, both in the short and long term.

Horsman Jr. periodically continued to travel to the Continent, though his trips now focused more on company business. He became aware of the work of early German doll artist Marion Kaulitz, founder of the so-called Puppenreform movement. Kaulitz, beginning about 1901, began designing dolls with realistic children's faces. It seems likely Horsman visited her doll

Billiken was Horsman's first successful Can't Break 'Em composition doll.

Horsman introduces Baby Bumps.

exhibit in Munich in 1909, and surely he was aware that German doll manufacturer, Kammer & Reinhardt joined the movement that year with the release of its first bisque-head "character" dolls designed by artists who modeled them after real children.

On his return to New York, Edward was determined that E.I. Horsman Co. would follow suit with a line of artistic character dolls with heads of Can't Break 'Em composition. In one of his most important decisions, he hired a young sculptress he had discovered, Helen Fox Trowbridge. Together, they would turn the American doll world upside down. During the decade, they were responsible for hundreds of successful composition dolls, not the least of which were the Campbell Kids, who remained a familiar and popular image through the rest of the twentieth century.

Horsman 1907 advertisement introduced Babyland Rag dolls with photo lithographed faces.

Seamstresses busily sewing clothes for the Horsman dolls manufactured by Aetna Doll and Toy Co.

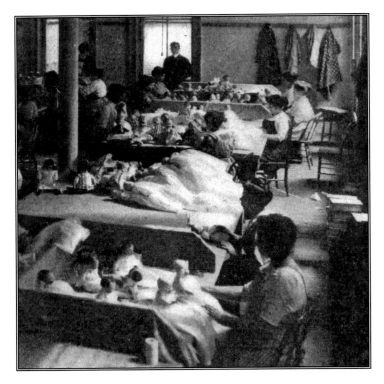

Women employees of Aetna Doll and Toy Co. dressing dolls.

A shipboard acquaintance snapped this photo of Horsman Jr. aboard the S.S. Pretoria during his trans-Atlantic crossing to Europe in June 1899.

During his visit to England in 1899, E.I. Horsman Jr., right, visited his friend, Edwin Lemare at Ventnor. Here the two friends pause a moment during a game of croquet.

Dolls of the Aughts

The Horsman company imported, assembled, and sold dolls since the 1870s. It seems likely that at least some from these early years must survive today. None of them, however, has been identified since it wasn't until about 1897 that the first Horsman dolls were brand marked.

In the early years of the twentieth century, *Playthings*, the new American toy industry's trade journal began publication. In the "aughts," the years from 1903 through 1910, the magazine's advertising and editorial pages helped make Horsman dolls a familiar name to department store buyers and toyshop retailers across the country.

BABYLAND RAG DOLLS — This series of cloth dolls probably was the first series of dolls popularly associated with the Horsman name. The first Horsman cloth doll that we know of to bear the Baby Land name (later the two words would be joined to form the more familiar Babyland name) appeared in the company's 1893 catalog. Babyland Rag dolls became a staple in Horsman's product line and remained there well into the 1920s. One series of such cloth dolls was known as American Maids.

The Babyland name continued in use until about 1928, although during the last several years, it was assigned to mama dolls with composition heads and limbs. These, of course, bore no resemblance to the earlier popular all-cloth Babyland Rag types.

The early versions had hand painted cloth faces, were jointed at shoulders and hips, and came in sizes from about 11" to 30". Some of these Babyland Rag dolls had mohair wigs; they were advertised as having clothes and could be dressed and undressed.

Between 1905 and 1907, several firms in Detroit, Michigan, began producing rag dolls with photogravure printed faces. Photographed images of actual babies and children were lithographed onto the flat cloth faces of the dolls. These were sold by Horsman competitors.

However, in 1907, Horsman followed suit and contracted with a supplier — it may have been one of the Michigan firms or, perhaps, Albert Bruckner, a New Jersey firm — to produce Babyland Rag dolls with "Life-Like" photograph faces. Horsman also continued to sell its original rag dolls with hand-painted faces for a number of years.

In 1911, it advertised 40 different styles of Babyland Rag dolls ranging in price from 25 cents to $5.

By 1912, Horsman was advertising a third style, which had a molded or pressed three-dimensional cloth face and lithographed features. These dolls, marked with the patent date of July 8, 1901, were made by the Bruckner firm.

One of the best known of the Babyland Rag dolls was **Topsy-Turvy**, a two-headed cloth doll. Turned one way, it was a white doll; turned upside down, with its skirt covering that face, it became a black doll.

There were literally dozens of different Babyland styles and sizes sold by Horsman over the years. They included **Sunbonnet Sue**, in dainty frock and sunbonnet; **Farm Boy Cy**, in overalls and shade hat; **Miss Priscilla**, wearing a gray Quaker's dress and kerchief; **Automobile Girl**, an "up-to-date" miss wearing a motorist's duster and a bonnet; **Little Bo Peep**, with her Dolly Varden costume; **Dutch Boy** and **Girl**, **Jan** and **Gretel**, wearing wooden shoes; **Golf Boy** and **Girl**, wearing hand knit sweaters, he in knickers, she with a broad hat.

Some other Babyland Rags were **Boy**, **Lady**, **American Maid**, **Big Baby**, **Fancy**, **Daisy**, **Clown**, **Dinah**, **Marjorie**, **Beauty**, **Red Riding Hood**, **Red Riding Hood Beauty**, **Tommy Tucker**, **Jack Robinson**, **Little Boy Blue**, and many more.

In 1914, Horsman also advertised **Stella**, a rag doll with the patented pressed fabric face, and **Nancy**, one of a line with celluloid faces. An earlier version of Stella with a flat hand-painted face, selling for 25 cents, was advertised as early as 1904.

A **Multi-face** rag doll, patented Jan. 3, 1913, was introduced in Horsman's catalog the next year. It had four separate lithographed faces that were interchangeable when the bonnet was removed and the dress yoke unhooked. The yoke, when replaced, hid the extra faces.

After 1912, the Babyland cloth line also featured several patented stuffed animals, including **Mary's Lamb** and **Mary's Puppy**. These infant's toys, 11½" tall, were unique in that their soft fleecy coat could be unsnapped, peeled off, and laundered. "At last, the up-to-date mother can realize her dream of a 'sterilized' plaything," its advertising read, "and the child can have a toy which each washing makes good as new." Trowbridge, who came up with the idea for these washable baby toys, told an interviewer years later that she had been particularly pleased with this innovation.

Big Babyland: 30", all original large Babyland Rag doll with hand-painted face. $2,500.00.
Courtesy Jean Grout.

Babyland Rag: 14", early doll with hand-painted face, original clothes, and blonde mohair wig. $850.00.
Courtesy Linda Edward, The Doll Museum.

Black Babyland: 14½", all-original with hand-painted face. $1,000.00. Courtesy Jean Grout.

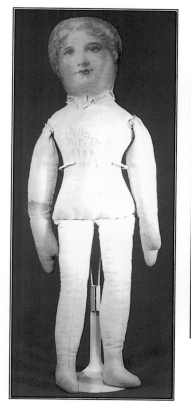

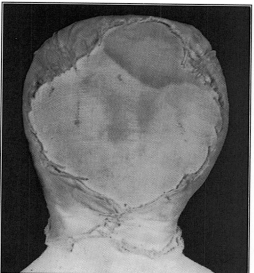

Litho Babyland: 14", Babyland Rag doll with Lifelike face. Note (rear view) the way the photo lithographed cloth face is sewn around the cloth head. The rear of the head would have been covered by a bonnet. $700.00. Courtesy Linda Edward, The Doll Museum.

Lifelike Litho: 14½", Babyland Rag with photographic printed face. $600.00. Courtesy Jean Grout.

Topsy-Turvy: 12", Babyland Rag with two lithographed faces, Little Eva (left) with printed blonde curls; turned upside-down (right) becomes Topsy, a black doll. $950.00. Courtesy Linda Edward, The Doll Museum.

Bruckner: 14", Topsy-Turvy two-headed doll with stiffened, molded mask-type faces made by Bruckner as part of Horsman's Babyland Rag series. $750.00.
Courtesy Jean Grout.

Series of Babyland Rag dolls as shown in a Horsman catalog, circa 1913.

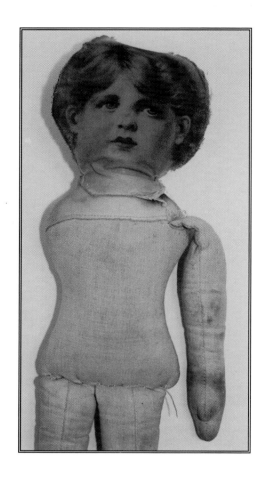

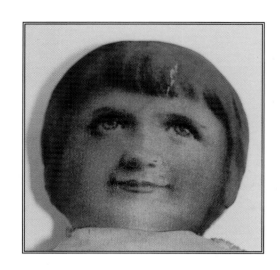

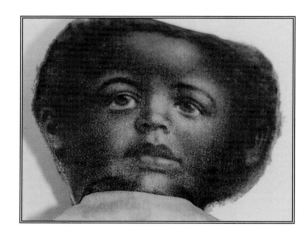

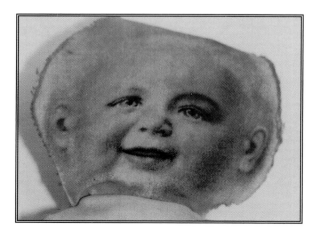

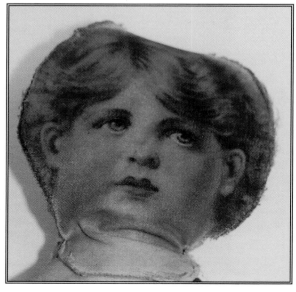

Multi-face: 14½", rare 1914 Babyland Rag doll has four separate flat, lithographed cloth faces. Missing arm. $150.00. Courtesy Jean Grout.

BEAUTY we call her,
      Beauty she is ;
Because of her clothes,
And her sweet little phiz.
Blue-eyed beauty
Do your duty,
Make the children happy, dear.
Who would want
A sweeter playmate ?
You are sure to bring good cheer.

No. 9—BABYLAND BEAUTY.

LITTLE Jack Horner sat in a corner,
      Eating his Xmas pie.
But little Jack Robinson,
With best bid and tucker on,
Stands ready for you to buy.

o. 14—BABYLAND, JACK ROBINSON.
Extra large—Same size as Dorothy.
Retails at $5.00

Fourteen of Horsman's Babyland Rag dolls, ranging in size from 13″ to 30″, were featured in a small color catalog distributed by Best & Co. department store, 60 – 62 West 23rd Street, New York, in the early years of the twentieth century.

HERE'S Dorothy, just the most lovely
of dolls.
As big as a two-year old.
Yet many a happy wee mother declares
She isn't too big to hold.

No. 15—BABYLAND, DOROTHY.
Extra large Size— 30 inches.
Retails at $3.98

Another Horsman's Babyland Rag dolls color catalog page.

Billiken.

BILLIKEN — While Horsman did not originate the teddy bear, the company was quick to climb on board the bandwagon and sold more than its share of the plush stuffed creatures. But as the teddy bear tide began to recede, the Horsmans, father and son, began looking around for the next big toy hit. They found it in Billiken, a curious-looking Oriental good luck charm with a watermelon grin.

The Billiken craze already was sweeping the U.S. The image was everywhere. There were Billiken statuettes, savings banks, paperweights, ink wells, calendars, clocks, writing pads, and picture frames. Early in 1909, Horsman signed a contract with Billiken Sales Co., of Chicago, for the exclusive right to make a Billiken doll.

Horsman had just entered into another agreement with Benjamin Goldenberg's Aetna Doll and Toy Co., to take the factory's entire production of unbreakable dolls. It instructed Aetna to make its Billiken with a Can't Break 'Em composition head on a plush teddy-bear-like body, with arms and legs jointed at the shoulders and hips.

Billiken was advertised as a "Teddy Doll," and in the next couple of years, Horsman reportedly sold a million of them, a remarkable toy success story. The doll came in 12" and 15" sizes.

In January 1910, Horsman ads featured a companion character called **Sister Billiken**. With a mohair wig and wearing a kimono, she came in the same sizes and was even more bizarre-looking than her "brother." Sister Billken was not a sales success.

Billiken: 11". Good luck mascot with jointed, stuffed plush body. $200.00. Courtesy Arlene Jensen.

Sister Billiken.

CHANTECLER — In 1910, Horsman introduced another fantastic creature, Chantecler, a colorful cloth rooster with a composition human head, made in two sizes. Chantecler, a vain cockerel, had his origins in a classic medieval tale and reappeared in French playwright Edmond Rostand's allegorical drama of the same name which opened to much fanfare that year. In Rostand's play, Chantecler and the other roles were played by actors in animal costumes, clearly the inspiration for the part-poultry, part-person design of the doll. Horsman's doll manufacturer, Aetna Doll and Toy Co. applied for a design trademark in March 1910, and it was registered as No. 78,390, on June 14. Rostand's experimental play quickly was judged a failure. Horsman's Chantecler must have been also. It is a very rare doll today.

Chantecler.

Baby Bumps.

BABY BUMPS — After Billiken, Baby Bumps became Horsman's second successful unbreakable composition doll and its first real character baby, the result of E.I. Horsman Jr.'s decision to shun the old fashioned "angel-faced" doll in favor of those modeled after real children. Baby Bumps, introduced in 1910, greatly resembles a well-known German bisque character face, Kammer & Reinhardt's No. 100 Baby. Soon, though, Horsman's designer, Helen Trowbridge would ignore German influence and create dozens of other dolls that were purely American in look.

Baby Bumps was one of a long series that the company would call "Art Dolls," a name coined by the artistically inclined Edward Horsman Jr., whose strong design ideas would guide the doll firm throughout most of the decade to come. As Horsman Jr. defined "Art Dolls," it meant they had been sculpted using real infants and children as models.

The Baby Bumps name, which would be used for years, was chosen to reflect that the doll's flange-neck Can't Break 'Em composition head could "take all kinds of bumps." Horsman would advertise in 1914 that its original unbreakable baby doll in four years had been "known...and loved...by more than a million children."

At first, Baby Bumps had a pink velvet body, stuffed with ground-cork, and paw-like hands. Later versions had sateen or muslin bodies and jointed sateen arms and legs. From 1911, some versions had composition hands. While most were white, a doll Horsman advertised as **Colored Baby Bumps** was sold. While the 12" and 14" sizes apparently were most popular, Baby Bumps came in sizes from the 9" **Baby Bumps Jr.** to the 18" **Big Baby Bumps**.

Although it had a different head, a doll called **Baby Blue**, "the Baby Beautiful," introduced by Horsman in 1910, also had a velvet body, albeit blue, not pink. This doll had blue eyes, wore a white gown with blue ribbons on the shoulders, and came in a blue box.

In 1914, Baby Bumps got a new face with a bit of a grin, also sculpted by Trowbridge. In 1916, there were versions called **Sandy Bumps** and **Mandy Bumps**, which came with their own small sand pails and shovels.

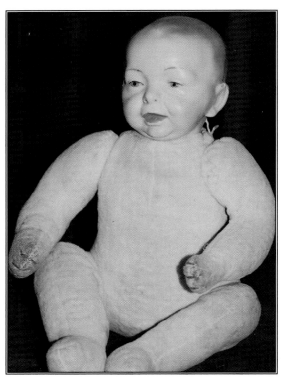

Baby Bumps: 11″, early Horsman doll with a Can't Break 'Em composition head on a stuffed plush body. $200.00. Courtesy Arlene Jensen.

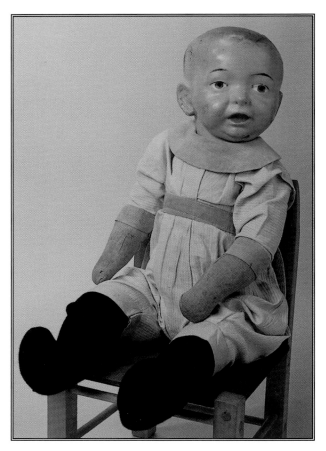

Baby Bumps: 18″, in original outfit. $200.00.

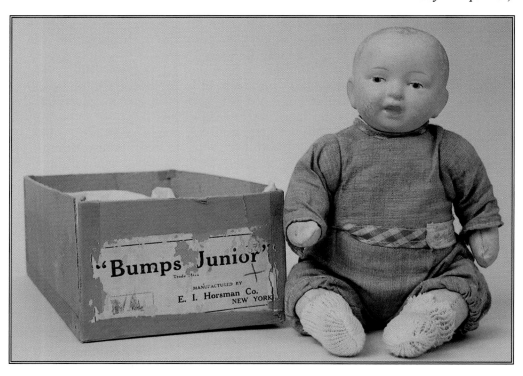

Baby Bumps Jr.: 9½″. $200.00.

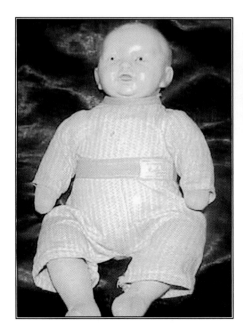

Baby Bumps: 10", early Horsman Can't Break 'Em doll with original tagged outfit. $250.00. Courtesy Dollies in the Big Apple.

Baby Bumps: 12", black version wearing original pink romper tagged "Genuine Baby Bumps — Trade mark." $350.00. Courtesy Dorothy Bohlin.

CAMPBELL KID — One of the best-known and loved dolls of all time is Horsman's Campbell Kid. Artist Grace Gebbie (Wiederseim) Drayton created the original illustrations of the cute and chubby soup-loving youngsters in 1905 for the Joseph Campbell Co. And in 1910, Campbell licensed Horsman to make and sell Campbell Kid dolls. E.I. Horsman Jr., listed on the patent application as the "inventor" of the dolls, instructed his chief designer Helen Fox Trowbridge to turn Drayton's two-dimensional drawings into a sculpted doll head. Later she would remark that since Drayton's illustrations included no profile views, she had to create the Campbell Kid's button nose without help from the artist. There is some evidence that she simply "exaggerated" a nose from one of her bas-relief medallions that she had sculpted of a baby during her pre-doll designing years. Clearly, her work has stood the test of time, and the cute and chubby soup-loving youngsters remain highly popular today.

The original Campbell Kids had Can't Break 'Em flange neck composition heads, cork stuffed pink sateen bodies, were jointed at the shoulders and hips and came in a number of different outfits and sizes, from 9½" to 16", the largest with composition legs. Some versions were wigged, some had painted hair; most had painted eyes that looked straight ahead, a rare few had side-glancing eyes. In 1914, Horsman brought out a head with a shoulder plate, allowing the doll to wear lower necked clothes.

An early favorite was the 1912 **Campbell Kid Mascot,** dressed in striped blazers of the colors of popular colleges. A curved-leg version was the **Campbell Kid Baby,** dressed in a slip with ribbon in her hair.

Over the years, Campbell Kids were dressed in a great many other costumes as well as clothes on which Horsman Jr. had taken out design patents. These included **Campbell Dutch Boy** and **Dutch Girl, Campbell Kid Cowboy, Cowgirl,** and **Baseball Kid.**

There was **Pocahontas,** and her boy companion, **Kickapoo,** described in Horsman's advertising as "attractive and comical little Indians." They were painted in brown-skin with black hair. Their painted eyes were shaped like hearts on their sides. The Indian dolls wore brown Indian costumes with red trim and red headbands with gaudy feathers.

In 1914, a French craze for colored hair was reflected in a number of Horsman dolls, including, of course, the Campbell Kids. For a brief time, they were available with red, blue, green or yellow wigs, in color-matching costumes and bows.

In 1928, another doll maker, American Character acquired the rights to use the Campbell Kid name and design. However, Horsman continued to produce composition dolls that while not identical, greatly resembled their traditional Campbell Kid, but were not identified or advertised as such. Horsman reacquired the licensing rights shortly after World War II and again began producing an authorized Campbell Kid doll.

Campbell Kid: 10", flared composition head, muslin body with inside disc joints at shoulders and hips. $350.00.

Campbell Kid: 10", in original outfit. $350.00.

Campbell Kid: 11", side-glancing girl in original tagged dress. $200.00. Courtesy Arlene Jensen.

Campbell Kids: 8½". Boy and girl pair. $500.00. Courtesy Sue Kinkade.

Campbell Kids: 15" (rear) $400; 10½" (front) $300.00; Pocahontas: 11" (left) $400.00.

Pocahontas: 11", Campbell Kid with brown-tone complexion. $350.00.

Indian Pair: 11", Campbell Kids as Kickapoo and Pocahontas. $700.00. Courtesy McMasters Doll Auction.

Mascot Boy: 11", Campbell Kid in collegiate outfit. Label on sleeve: "The Campbell Kids // Trade Mark // Copyright Campbell Company // Mfg. By E. Horsman Co." $250.00.

Dutch Campbell Kid: 16", in original outfit. $350.00.

Campbell Kid Baby.

Other related Drayton-designed Horsman dolls included **Gee Gee Dolly**, copyrighted in 1912, a 16" cloth doll version with a composition mask face. Late in 1913, this doll was renamed **Peek-a-Boo**, but it soon evolved in a number of different ways, including all composition and composition-and-cloth versions, with distinctive star-like hands. Peek-A-Boo came in a number of sizes, some as small as 7½".

Some of Drayton's cute creations were four-legged. In 1911 and for at least several years after, Horsman sold **Puppy Pippin** and his feline companion, **Pussy Pippin.** They were described in Horsman's advertising as "The Campbell Kids of the animal world…having heads of our celebrated Can't Break 'Em material, and bodies of fine velvet matching the head coloring. The legs are jointed." These animals came in two sizes, standard and a smaller 11" junior. The compo heads and stuffed tail were sewn to the plush body; Puppy Pippin had a wide collar.

Peek-A-Boo.

Peek-A-Boo: 8", jointed only at the shoulders. $95.00.

Puppy Pippin and Pussy Pippin.

Puppy Pippin: 11". $400.00.

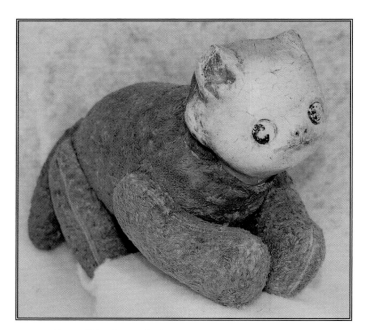

Pussy Pippin: 11". $350.00. Courtesy Julie Ghavam.

Several years later, Horsman added two more of Drayton's animal creations, **Frisky Fido** and **Precious Pussy**. Unlike the Pippin duo, these 12" characters stood upright, not on all fours. They had flange-neck unbreakable composition heads with protruding, molded tongues, cloth bodies, and inside-jointed limbs. A 1915 ad described Fido as "a new creation by Mrs. Drayton." He was dressed in cotton blouse with bow tie and striped knickers. Precious Pussy was dressed in an attractive skirt, looking for all the world like "the original innocent pussy that ate the canary."

Frisky Fido: 12", Drayton design. $200.00.

In addition to the Drayton-designed cats and dogs, Horsman also produced several other animal dolls. They included **Teddy Bull Moose.** In the months before the presidential election of 1912, the company apparently counted on Theodore Roosevelt's new progressive Bull Moose Party to return the ex-president to the White House. With this expectation, the company brought out Teddy Bull Moose, a doll reminiscent of Puppy and Pussy Pippin, which combined composition heads and stuffed velour bodies with jointed limbs. The doll had a unique and quite realistic sculpted moose head, complete with rack of antlers. "The Craze," Horsman's advertising claimed, "a ready-made demand for it the country over." The *New York Herald,* two months before the election, announced that "Teddy Bull Moose has routed Teddy Bear…he is the monarch of all the toys." Both Horsman and the *Herald* were wrong. Roosevelt lost, and Teddy Bull Moose was a sales failure. It is a very rare doll today.

Towzer appeared on the toy market around 1914. A very rare doll today, he had a bulldog's molded composition head and a plush stuffed body of fine velvet. He was fully jointed and wore a studded leather collar. **Co-Co-Da-Monk** also dates to about 1914 and was a cloth-bodied organ grinder's monkey with a Can't Break 'Em composition head. Designed by an unnamed "good artist," possibly Trowbridge, he came in two sizes, 12" and 17". Co-co wore a red and blue suit, advertised as "cut by the best monkey-tailor in Toyland," and a leather collar with chain attached.

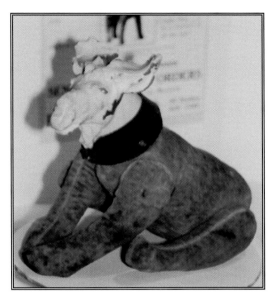

Teddy Bull Moose: 11". $500.00.

Dr. Cook and Lt. Peary.

HORSMAN'S "COOK" and "PEARY" DOLLS

LIFELIKE REPRESENTATIONS
of the
EXPLORERS

From Models Made by
an Eminent Sculptor

Protected by Design Patents

Size, 12 inches   Each in a box
Per dozen, $8.50

Dr. Cook.   Lieut. Peary.

ESKIMO DOLLS – In 1909, Horsman advertised a series of Eskimo dolls dressed in pseudo-fur mohair parkas and hoods. These included two early celebrity dolls, **Dr. Cook** and **Lt. Peary**. These dolls represented Arctic explorers F.A. Cook and Robert Edwin Peary. In April 1909, Peary was acclaimed when he became the first man to reach the North Pole. Belatedly, Cook claimed to have beaten him to the Arctic goal the previous year. Although Cook's claim later was discredited, at the time these dolls were released, he, like Peary, was considered an American hero. Horsman's advertising does not say whether these 12-inch dolls were composition. More likely they were bisque dolls made in Germany.

Junior Takes Charge

Edward I. Horsman Sr., about 65 years old.

On May 12, 1909, Florence B. Horsman died at the age of 61. In the months following her death, E.I. Horsman Sr., her husband of 40 years, was seriously depressed, and his son feared for his physical health as well. Junior persuaded his father to take a long vacation abroad.

On Jan. 8, 1910, Horsman Sr. set sail for Egypt on the first real vacation he had ever taken. By all accounts, the foreign travel medicine worked. He was enthusiastic about Egypt, "its wonderful climate and bright skies with never a cloud, its glorious sunsets and afterglow on the deserts."

After two weeks in Cairo, he took a 20-day trip up the Nile to Luxor and the great dam under construction at Aswan. Then he sailed to Italy and spent several weeks in Venice before heading to Monte Carlo and the French Riviera. Long stays, first in Paris and then in London, completed Horsman's four-month sojourn abroad.

E.I. Horsman Sr., on donkey, visiting Egypt in 1910.

E.I. Horsman Sr. feeding pigeons in St. Mark's Square in Venice during his first long vacation abroad.

All the while, Junior was taking care of business back in New York, and proving himself a fully capable leader of the E.I. Horsman Co. during his father's prolonged absence.

By 1912, Aetna's 35,000 square foot factory was turning out seven dolls a minute, 3,800 dolls each 9-hour work day, nearly a million dolls a year, all for Horsman.

American doll manufacturers regularly complained that their German competitors employed an army of ill-paid peasant families to paint, sew, and finish dolls on a piecework basis in their own homes. And it is true that German manufacturers were able to deliver their dolls at cheap prices because of their exploited cottage industry work force. The dirty little secret though is that U.S. doll makers, including Aetna, did something very similar.

According to Miriam Formanek-Brunell, writing about child labor in turn-of-the-century New York City, many immigrant families — 70 percent of them recently arrived from Italy — were employed in this doll homework. Whole families, parents and children, worked in their dark, crowded, and often cold tenement flats, sewing limbs and bodies for Campbell Kid dolls and the outfits to dress them. Working at piecework rates, children as young as 4 stitched and stuffed for seven or more hours a day to earn a few dollars weekly to help supplement the family's meager income.

One manufacturer — it may have been Aetna — reported to the New York State Department of Labor in 1912 that the company did not investigate the homes where some of its doll work was done. The doll company's representative told investigators he'd never checked the conditions under which its doll outfits were made.

As deplorable as this may seem today, it should be noted that child labor was by no means limited to the toy industry in the early twentieth century, and that many families considered it an absolute necessity to survive. It should be noted, too, that seven decades later, Horsman would be among the last American doll makers to end production in the

Edward I. Horsman Jr., in his 30s, after joining his father's firm, E.I. Horsman Co., as vice president.

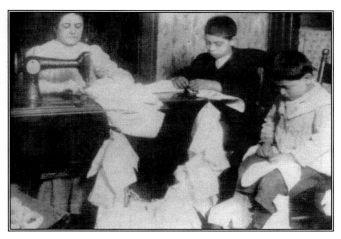

Whole familes of newly arrived immigrants, working in their crowded tenement flats, sewed cloth bodies and clothes for New York City dollmakers, including Horsman's supplier, Aetna Doll and Toy Co., in the early 1900s.

Artists are shown painting features on the doll heads. The photo was taken in 1912 in the Aetna Doll and Toy Co. factory in New York City.

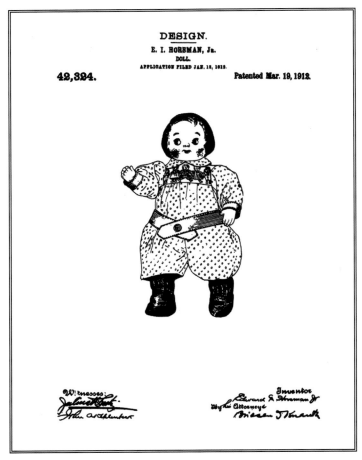

Edward I. Horsman Jr. is listed on these design patents as the "inventor" of the dolls that would become famous as the Campbell Kids.

U.S. because it could no longer compete with much lower Third World labor costs. In 1913, New York did pass a law prohibiting the home manufacture of dolls and dolls' clothing.

The next several years brought further improvements to Horsman's line of dolls. Horsman Jr. applied for and received design patents for attractive new outfits for the popular Campbell Kids. New doll faces were modeled by Trowbridge and several other sculptors, including a young Bernard Lipfert. A new "velvet" finish was developed for the Can't Break 'Em composition, and as the company advertised, an "exquisite skin coloring that can only be compared to that of healthy childhood which it so well represents."

On July 3, 1914, Junior returned from another of his extended business and pleasure trips to various cities on the Continent. With him he brought sketches of new French fashions. A promotional article soon appeared in *Playthings*, noting a new line of dolls dressed in frocks that are "absolutely the last word

Horsman's Campbell Kids got a publicity boost when this kick-line chorus, decked out in doll-like masks and costumes, toured the country performing in the musical comedy, "Merry, Merry."

Helen Trowbridge worked from Drayton's two-dimensional sketches to create the cute and chubby Campbell Kid dolls.

from Paris in doll costumes…replicas of costumes taken from life by Mr. E.I.H. Jr., on his last trip abroad."

In October 1915, to mark the company's Golden Anniversary, the Horsman company announced it would move its showrooms and offices from Broadway to the former Tiffany Building on Manhattan's Union Square. The move was made the day after Christmas, and the new headquarters building was impressive.

The first floor showroom was 150 feet long, 75 feet wide, with a pressed tin ceiling 22 feet high. There were ten beautiful pure white Corinthian columns. Down the center of the room was a massive row of tall, glass-front white showcases with 230 different Horsman dolls displayed. Other toys and novelties in the company's product line were displayed on tables flanking the doll cabinets. Monster dollhouses, home to more of the character and art dolls, were arrayed on the mezzanine. Presiding over the large salesroom at what he called the "firing line" desk was Edward Horsman Jr., ready to greet visiting department store buyers as they came in the door.

In 1916, the company began switching its doll molding process from the cold-poured Can't Break 'Em material to the new hot-pressed wood-fiber type composition that was lighter in weight, nearly as durable, cheaper, and

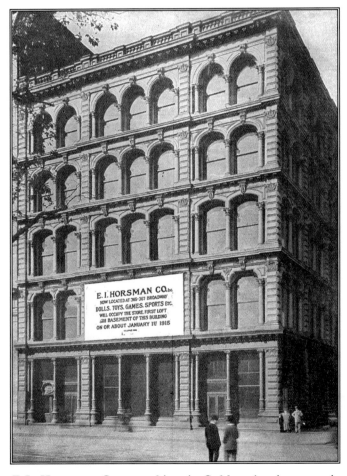

E.I. Horsman Co., marking is Golden Anniversary in 1915, moved into spacious new quarters in the former Tiffany Building on Union Square in New York City.

In the new Horsman showrooms, tall glass-front cases displayed 230 different dolls.

Ten white Corinthian columns dominated the 150-foot first floor showroom.

more efficient to make. It was advertised as Adtocolite. At first the new composition was used only for heads, but as the new molding techniques improved, Horsman came out with an all-composition doll — head, body and limbs — in early 1918.

This all-compo doll "is really worthy to take its place among the other Horsman dolls," pronounced Junior.

Babyland Rag dolls that had been in the company's line for more than two decades got a new burst of energy when Trowbridge turned her restless energy toward designing cloth dolls.

Things seemed to be going wonderfully well for the E.I. Horsman Co., but, then, on Saturday afternoon, July 27, 1918, 45-year-old Edward Horsman Jr. collapsed while working in the garden of his rented summer home in Summit, New Jersey.

His wife, Ethel was nearby and saw him fall. She summoned help, but her husband had been stricken with a fatal heart attack. Two days later, after a funeral at his home at 152 West 57th Street in New York City, he was buried in the family plot in Brooklyn's Green-Wood Cemetery, beside his infant son and only child, Edward I. Horsman III, who had died in infancy some 13 years earlier. Ethel survived her husband by 15 years. She died January 21, 1933, at the age of 59.

"The industry will sorely miss him," *Playthings* eulogized, "as he was one of those men to whom all who knew him looked for great things, and he never disappointed these expectations.

"Enthusiastic to a great degree, thoroughly American in all his aims and ideals, and bearing a name which has been honored in the history of the American toy trade for over a half century, his loss will be felt now and in the future!"

From his "firing line" desk, E.I. Horsman Jr. presided over the large salesroom.

Dolls Face a New Look

One morning in the autumn of 1909, Edward Horsman Jr. had been stopped in his tracks by something he'd spotted in the window of Brentano's bookstore, a display of medallions — low-relief sculpted plaques — of children's faces.

Earlier, the E.I. Horsman Co. had negotiated exclusive rights to a remarkable doll-making material, and its first Can't Break 'Em composition head good luck charm, the Buddha-like Billiken, was a smash hit. Now Horsman Jr. hoped to follow that success with a whole new line of unbreakable composition children's dolls.

Here, he thought, was an artist whose arresting bas-relief clay images caught the very essence of the American child, a person who could design the character doll heads he hoped to put on the market. Edward Horsman turned and walked into the shop. Inquiry soon took him to the portrait medallionist, Helen Fox Trowbridge.

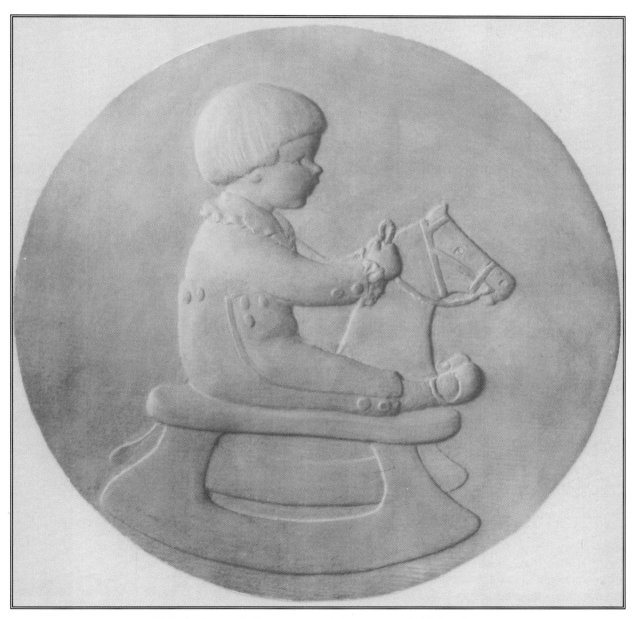

Helen's clay medallions captured the essence of childhood.

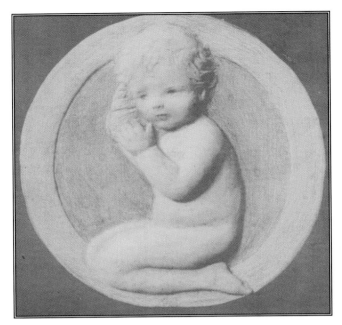

Helen's bas relief medallions in a shop window caught the attention of E.I. Horsman Jr.

In 1909, there was virtually no U.S. doll industry. Bisque-head dolls, imported from Germany, dominated the playthings market. But Helen Trowbridge would change that. By the time the sculptress modeled her last prototype for the Horsman company in the early 1920s, American-made composition dolls were well established; the German monopoly was shattered.

Trowbridge, with her innovative and delightfully designed character doll faces, may be fairly considered as one of the most important but least appreciated contributors to the establishment of the early American toy industry. In little more than a decade, this talented sculptress designed scores of charming dolls. Because her designs — most of them produced in Horsman's patented "Can't Break 'Em" composition — so caught the public's fancy, they altered forever a child's idea of what a dolly should look like.

Born in New York City, Sept. 19, 1882, Helen was the daughter of Dr. George H. and Harriet Gibbs Fox. Her lineage was long and prominent. On her father's side, the Fox family traces its history to the eighth century and Charlemagne. The Gibbs line goes back nearly as far — an ancestor, Saire de Quincy's name is on the Magna Carta — and is said to include crowned heads of a half-dozen European nations.

Helen Fox Trowbridge.

Helen's childhood centered on the Fox family's four-story home at 18 East 31st Street, between Manhattan's Fifth and Madison Avenues. She grew up in a world of brownstone houses, like her own, with streets paved with Belgian blocks and filled with clip-clopping horse-drawn vehicles. In summer, Helen's world expanded to include the homes of relatives and friends living mostly in western New York State, New Jersey, and Connecticut.

Years later, Helen would recall her birthday in September 1885.

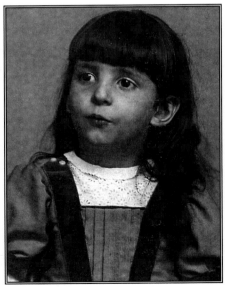

Helen's childhood centered on the Fox family's New York City brownstone home.

"On my third birthday…we were visiting at the time in my mother's old home in Nunda (a small town in western New York)…. I was having my lunch alone in the cool, dark dining room…when there came a knock on the side screen of the room. It was a package the postman had brought for Miss Helen Fox. My mother, who was (at home) in New York attending to housepainters, had sent me a doll in my first parcel."

From childhood, Helen demonstrated a talent for art and modeling, delighting in making figures from clay.

At 16, Helen went away to a Connecticut boarding school.

Helen was schooled at home by a tutor until she was nine, then was sent to a nearby private school. At 16, she went away to Ingleside, a boarding school at New Milford, Connecticut. Later she would say that she received a proper finishing school education there, meaning her education was expected to end with graduation. Nonetheless, she decided to pursue her longtime artistic interests.

She began her studies in October 1900 at New York's Art Students' League, but soon was discouraged. Her drawing was stiff and mechanical, she felt, inferior to most of the other students. Several months later, prematurely conceding defeat, she changed course, deciding to be a chemistry teacher. But there, too, she found herself ill-prepared by her finishing school education. She dropped out and, as did so many other affluent young people of the time, traveled to Europe. It was a summer of fun and adventure, but also it gave her time to "find" herself.

When she returned home that fall, her goal was set. She resumed her art studies and quickly rediscovered her childhood enthusiasm for three-dimensional modeling. She studied at the New York School of Applied Design,

then apprenticed with the talented American sculptor, Gutzon Borglum, who later would carve the massive features of four former U.S. presidents on South Dakota's Mount Rushmore.

In New York, Helen launched her sculpting career. She visited hospital maternity wards, sketching newborns whose portraits she later would render as clay medallions, some of which also would be cast in bronze. She spotted other subjects, young children of all races and nationalities on the streets of Manhattan. With her "portable studio," Helen was a common sight in the multi-ethnic, working class East Side neighborhoods.

In June 1909, she married Mason Trowbridge, a rising young attorney she had met four years earlier during a Yale football weekend. That was the same year she was contacted by Horsman Jr. Would she create character doll faces modeled from real, live American children? At first she hesitated. Redirecting her focus from portrait sculpting to toymaking was an unsettling choice for a serious artist. But, as she would admit in a newspaper article some years later, she was ready for a new challenge. Her answer was yes.

After their wedding, Helen and Mason Trowbridge moved into a $50-a-month rented bungalow on Vanderventer Avenue in nearby Port Washington, Long Island. There they became good friends of a young couple living across the street, Hal and Grace Lewis. Soon, the rest of the world would know Hal by his name on the cover of his bestselling novels, Sinclair Lewis.

Helen Fox Trowbridge with a niece and nephew on her wedding day.

Helen, husband Mason Trowbridge, and their six children. Eventually she would give up creating Horsman's dolls to devote more time to her family.

Lewis would pen an affectionate inscription on the flyleaf of one of his first editions: "To the Trowbridges, who took both the 'nay' and the 'bores' out of the once dreaded word, 'neighbors'...."

Of Helen, Grace Lewis later would say, soon she was "producing babies with speed and casualness." Her first child, Mason Jr., was born in 1910. Harriet was born in 1912; George, in 1916; Adaline, the following year; and James, in 1920. The Trowbridge's sixth and last child, Cornelia, was born in 1922.

Shortly after her marriage, Helen set up a small studio in her Port Washington home and began sculpting dolls for Horsman.

In 1910, the company followed up on Billiken with its first real character doll, Baby Bumps, the result of Horsman's decision to shun the old-fashioned, sweet but vapid-looking German "dolly" faces. But with Baby Bumps, the company still hadn't broken free of the Teutonic influences, the doll bearing a resemblance to a Kammer & Reinhardt character baby.

In introducing it, Horsman carefully chose a name that would emphasize that the doll's unbreakable composition head could "take all kinds of bumps."

It is uncertain if the original Baby Bumps was Helen's work, but she did sculpt a number of variations in subsequent years. These included a 9" Baby Bumps Jr.; a 17" nearly life-sized infant and, in 1914, a slightly older Baby Bumps with a more grown-up smile and side-glancing eyes.

Perhaps Helen's most successful doll head was the classic Campbell Kid, the cute and chubby little face that launched a billion bowls of vegetable soup. However, she received little credit for her sculpture since she had worked from the two-dimensional sketches — none, though, that showed a profile view — that Grace Gebbie Wiederseim (Drayton) had drawn for the Joseph Campbell Company.

In fact, for a time, though she'd designed literally dozens of character dolls for Horsman, the company itself didn't publicly acknowledge her identity, referring to her, generically, as "an American sculptress." But her talented eye and hands couldn't long be denied and before long, the name Helen Trowbridge was appearing on Horsman's design patent applications.

Of these early Can't Break 'Em character dolls, one that seemed to stand out in her later recollections was the head she sculpted in 1911 using her own one-year-old son, Mason Jr., as the model. It was the first in a series that Horsman called the Gold Medal Baby.

Many of Trowbridge's realistic infants appeared in Horsman's Nature Baby collection. One of these dolls, which also debuted in 1911, was called Baby Suck-A-Thumb, a curious name, since, because of the size and shape of its fingers, it could not! Helen rectified that problem with another doll in the Gold Medal Baby

Helen Trowbridge, ready for a new challenge, chose to switch from serious portrait sculpting to modeling doll faces.

series, which was introduced for the 1914 Christmas season. Called, simply, Suck-A-Thumb, it had side-glancing eyes and hair molded in a bit of a topknot, with an open mouth and patented right arm and hand designed so as to simulate thumb sucking.

Although by this time Trowbridge had sculpted many composition heads for Horsman, it was her novel Suck-A-Thumb that finally brought her real public attention. She was featured, along with other doll artists such as Margarete Steiff, Kathe Kruse, and Rose O'Neill, in a *New York Herald* article titled, "Sisters of Santa Claus," which appeared shortly before Christmas.

"Between her love for her children and that of her work of toy modeling, Mrs. Helen Fox Trowbridge scarcely knows which makes her happiest," the newspaper story said. That she was able to do much of her sculpting at home meant that she didn't have to make the tough choice between working and being a stay-at-home Mom. Not surprisingly, therefore, the article noted that she was a "strong advocate of specialized home industries for women."

The *Herald* article makes it clear that Helen continued to find other artistic outlets, both commercial and purely personal, besides sculpting dolls.

"Not satisfied with merely making dolls for Santa Claus' pack, you may find Mrs. Trowbridge almost any day, when Jack Frost is not too active, sitting in her garden working on other things for children — book plates for the first library, wallpaper designs for children's rooms, silhouettes and patented sanitary detachable covers for wooly lambs. She does statues of children at rest, children at play and at study."

Although by 1916, Horsman was utilizing other sculptors — including a young Bernard Lipfert, who had graduated from painting doll heads for Horsman to modeling them — Helen was still the firm's chief designer. It was a position she would maintain for at least several more years.

Suck-a-Thumb, a novel Trowbridge design, had a molded topknot, open mouth, and thumb to suck.

A bearded Horsman Jr. is framed by a porthole during a trans-Atlantic crossing.

A week before Christmas, 1918, the *New York Evening Sun* ran a story headlined "If All Doll-Babies Don't Look Alike to You…Thanks Are Due to a Woman Sculptor."

It was Helen Fox Trowbridge, the article explained, who was "responsible for the transformation" to composition dolls which were more human, with "emotions and feelings to show like really-for-true babies."

Trowbridge was interviewed in a small room in Horsman's wholesale house on lower Broadway, where she was putting the "finishing touches" on a clay model of a two-year-old toddler. While it isn't possible now to determine which doll this became, the reporter called it "different from any you have ever seen and more like a real child than any other. The expression is that of a youngster suddenly taken by surprise. The lips are half parted, the eyes wide open with delight, the soft cheeks just beginning to bulge with a coming smile.

"What I want to do," Helen explained, "is to get the makers to turn them out more in the proportions of real children. But it is hard to make a superintendent of a doll factory understand that it is desirable to make a baby doll with arms that extend below the waistline, or with legs in true physiological proportions to the body. They have never done it. Therefore they will not believe that any one really wants them to do it save, perhaps, an exceptional artist with ideas unshared by the juvenile public!"

Had Helen Trowbridge moved too far and too fast for Horsman or any toy company? It seemed so.

"What I want to do," she said, "is to get back to my real work, the work I left to do this; the work that is better and more worthwhile and what I started in the first place to do."

But then, the newspaper article continued, her ambivalence became apparent. A certain light came into her eyes. She paused, and continued, quietly: "But it's the hardest thing to drag yourself away from these!"

After this, Helen Trowbridge designed few new composition dolls. But one of them clearly was a favorite, the Jackie Coogan Kid, her only celebrity doll. Charlie Chaplin discovered young Jackie, then only 4, in 1917. After appearing in a series of silent shorts, he found stardom in 1921 as the quintessential waif, playing opposite the great Chaplin in "The Kid."

The 7-year-old boy was a smash hit, and Horsman quickly signed a licensing agreement to produce a Jackie Coogan Kid doll. Trying to cash in quickly, the dollmaker redressed an existing doll, one that had been on the market for seven years, and called it Jackie Coogan. But that was just a stopgap.

Trowbridge was commissioned to do a new doll head, one that looked like the child star, complete with his Dutch boy haircut. Young Coogan actually sat for Helen who made sketches and measurements. Though the result was a remarkable likeness, Horsman felt it made The Kid look "too shrewd and too old a type to be pleasing." The likeness was modified to make a more pleasing doll.

One of the last of Trowbridge's composition dolls was Bye Bye Baby, a unique doll whose arms could, with the pull of a string, move in a lifelike manner, imitating a baby's gestures. It was made of Adtocolite, Horsman's

Rare original sketches by Helen Trowbridge who discovered she preferred designing cloth dolls and outfits to sculpting clay.

Flowered cotton crêpe dress.
Rose colored linen jacket.
Feather-stitched patch.

name for the improved hot pressed wood fiber composition, which, a half dozen years earlier, had replaced the old Can't Break 'Em type compo. The new material and technique allowed the company to produce better dolls faster and cheaper than before.

But Helen, by her own description, always "a designing fool," hadn't abandoned an interest in creating dolls. For some time she had been intrigued by the possibilities posed by cloth dolls. Even as a child, she had created rag dolls for herself and her young friends.

In 1918, after the Trowbridges had moved to Upper Montclair, New Jersey, she designed a cloth baby doll with painted face. She recruited local high school girls to cut and sew the dolls. The project gained momentum, a work-room was rented, and hundreds of dolls were produced. They were sold, with the profits being contributed to a wartime charitable fund directed by author Edith Wharton. Horsman later took over Helen's project, paying a percentage of each sale to the war relief fund. Helen continued to design new cloth dolls for Horsman's Babyland Rag series, which continued into the 1920s.

Tell mother these Horsman dolls are "made in a big, airy, sanitary factory," this 1917 advertisement urged children.

Part of Horsman's 1918 line-up of dolls was pictured in this magazine advertisement.

In a 1936 newspaper article, Helen said: "It is very funny, but I like to maintain I am the only woman who at one time earned a living by not knowing how to sew. I began to work on the rag doll design and hadn't the faintest idea how to cut a sleeve. I had to design it so simply that it was no effort for the operators to turn out, consequently it was most successful."

Her rag doll Patty-Cake was distributed by Horsman for about eight years, with variations known as Baby Patty-Cake and Pat-A-Cake, which allowed the child to insert a hand in the back of the doll to make it clap in delight. In 1922, Trowbridge was issued a design patent, which she then assigned to Horsman, for another rag doll with yarn hair and side-glancing eyes. With that, though, she seemingly ended her commercial doll-designing career, although she would continue to promote homemade craft toys for the rest of her life.

In 1916, Mason Trowbridge had left his law practice and joined toothpaste and soap maker Colgate. He would be associated with Colgate as the corporation's general counsel until his retirement. Over the years, the family lived in Port Washington, then moved to Glen Ridge, New Jersey, then, to nearby Upper Montclair. Later the Trowbridges would live in Chicago for a half dozen years, but then returned to New Jersey.

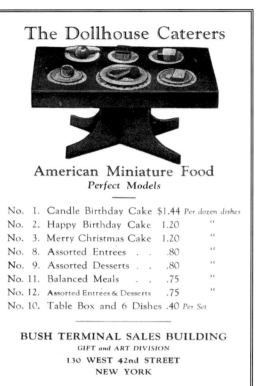

The Dollhouse Caterers

American Miniature Food
Perfect Models

No.	1.	Candle Birthday Cake	$1.44 *Per dozen dishes*
No.	2.	Happy Birthday Cake	1.20 "
No.	3.	Merry Christmas Cake	1.20 "
No.	8.	Assorted Entrees . .	.80 "
No.	9.	Assorted Desserts . .	.80 "
No.	11.	Balanced Meals . .	.75 "
No.	12.	Assorted Entrées & Desserts	.75 "
No.	10.	Table Box and 6 Dishes	.40 *Per Set*

BUSH TERMINAL SALES BUILDING
GIFT and ART DIVISION
130 WEST 42nd STREET
NEW YORK

In the 1930s, Helen modeled and sold dolly-sized foods and dollhouse accessories.

Helen launched a new venture in 1934, making and selling in a New York shop miniature dollhouse accessories. She fashioned wee potted plants, sets of alphabet blocks small enough for a doll to play with, scaled-down tables and lamps, even a tiny candle that glowed. She particularly enjoyed creating mini meals, more than 30 different kinds of dolly-sized foods, everything from plaster pies to casseroles of browned baked beans — painted birdseed, actually. Though unique, this business survived only a few years.

Mason retired in 1946, and the couple moved to an apartment in Manhattan. In 1954, the couple moved to West Cornwall, Connecticut. In March 1962, Mason died at the age of 84. Helen survived him by eight years. On July 27, 1970, she died following a short illness. She was 87. Survivors included four of her children and 12 grandchildren.

Her death went unnoticed by the huge American toy industry that her early work had helped to spawn. A tiny obituary in the *New York Times* noted merely that "Mrs. Trowbridge, the former Helen Fox, designed dolls for Horsman Dolls."

In retirement, Helen Trowbridge lived quietly in Connecticut. She died in 1970 at the age of 87.

Horsman's Other Designers

There were similarities between Helen Fox Trowbridge and Laura Gardin, two women sculptors who designed dolls for Horsman during the second decade of the twentieth century.

Both grew up and were educated in New York City, although Gardin was seven years younger. Both received artistic training at New York's Art Students' League. Both were little-known artists in their 20s when art enthusiast Edward Horsman Jr., spotted their talent and commissioned them to model doll heads for E.I. Horsman Co.

And while both abandoned doll designing rather early — Gardin after only a handful of dolls and several years — their lives then took widely divergent paths. Trowbridge left her art career to concentrate on a growing family. Gardin — by then Laura Gardin Fraser — had no children and focused, instead, on a sculpting career that grew ever more illustrious.

Born in Chicago, Sept. 14, 1889, Laura was the daughter of John Emil and Alice (Tilton) Gardin. Her mother was a noted watercolorist who founded an art school. The family moved to New York City, where Laura attended the Horace Mann School. In 1907, at the age of 18, she entered the Art Students' League, and became the pupil of sculpting instructor James Earle Fraser.

Fraser, best known for his design of the U.S. "Buffalo nickel" in 1913, had been a protégé and associate of the famed sculptor Augustus St. Gaudens. When his mentor died in 1907, Fraser, 31, began teaching at the Art Students' League. One of his first students, and the most talented, was Laura Gardin. She studied with him for three years, the only instructor she ever had. And, three years later in 1913, they married.

It was in about 1912 that Gardin's work came to the attention of Edward Horsman Jr., probably through his art world connections and Fraser. She was hired to create heads for the doll company. How many she modeled for Horsman in 1912 and 1913 is not known, but three were copyrighted with her name as the designer. They were identified as Merry Max, a laughing baby; Eric, a child with short, molded hair, and one called Peter Pan. It is likely, though, that Horsman sold composition dolls with these faces under various other names.

Laura soon returned to sculpting more serious subjects, including the mythological "Nymph and Satyr," now in the Metropolitan Museum of Art in New York. In 1916 it won her the first of many major awards, the Barnett prize of the National Academy of Design. After serving in the Army ambulance corps during WWI, she resumed an art career that would span another half-century.

She sculpted heroic-sized statues and fountains for outdoor sites, but she became best known as a medallist and received commissions and won competitions for many commemorative ones. These included the George Washington Bicentennial medal and a Congressional medal honoring Charles Lindbergh's 1927 trans-Atlantic flight. Also, in the 1930s, she designed three commemorative 50-cent pieces for the U.S. Mint and coins for the Philippines.

Her "Better Babies" medal, created for a *Woman's Home Companion* award, showed a pair of happy chubby babies seated on the floor. This and a number of other works depicting children and, especially, small animals led one art historian to note, "It is the young of the species that are of special interest to Mrs. Fraser."

In their Westport, Connecticut, studios, she and her husband enjoyed a very successful artistic partnership. In 1953, he died, but his widow continued to sculpt. Her last work was unveiled in June 1966, three large bronze panels depicting the history of America for the U.S. Military Academy, West Point. Just two months later, on Aug. 13, 1966, Laura Gardin Fraser died of a stroke. She was 77.

Sculptor Ernesto Peruggi, designer of Horsman's teenage Sweetheart dolls.

Ernesto Peruggi was a sculptor better known in doll circles than the art world. Though a talented artist, his reputation seems to have been regional, in the New York and New Jersey area, rather than national.

He was born in Naples, Italy, in 1884, and, a 1920 *Playthings* article said that he "showed signs in early child-

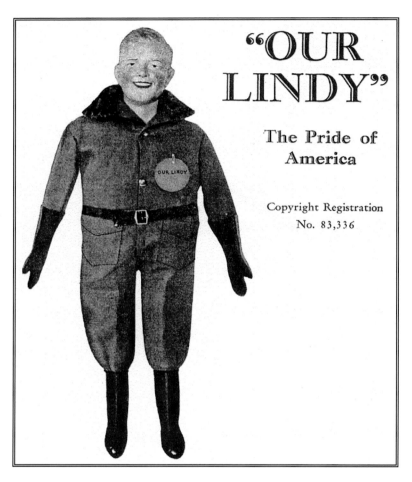

"OUR LINDY"

The Pride of America

Copyright Registration No. 83,336

In 1926, Ernesto Peruggi sculpted a remarkable likeness of trans-Atlantic aviator Charles Lindberg for Regal's Our Lindy doll.

hood of the talents that later shaped the course of his life work." In his native land, he graduated from the Academie Belle Arti and emigrated to the U.S. sometime after about 1910. In 1915, he designed a series of eight dolls for the Trion Toy Company. In the late teens and 1920s, he modeled heads for a number of doll companies, including Daniel Pollack, American Bisque Doll Company, Manhattan Toys and Dolls Manufacturing Company, Fine Doll Manufacturing Company, and Novelty Doll Company.

In 1923, he resculpted Effanbee's popular Baby Grumpy, and two years later, modeled a newborn infant for the same firm, a doll that probably was later produced as Pat-o-Pat.

In 1926, Peruggi designed several newborn babies for Regal Doll Manufacturing Co., but one of his best-known dolls today is Our Lindy, a realistic likeness of the boyish Charles Lindbergh which Regal released in 1928, a year after the intrepid aviator crossed the Atlantic alone.

As far as is known, no Horsman dolls were sculpted by Peruggi prior to the early 1930s, when Regal acquired the Horsman company. In 1938, though, he created Horsman's Sweetheart, a series inspired by Effanbee's success with the Dewees Cochran American Children, but surely distinctive in its own right.

A *Playthings* advertisement in September of that year called Sweetheart "a true reproduction of girls between the ages of ten and sixteen. They are dressed in the latest fashions. The characters are sculptured by the famous sculptor Ernesto Peruggi. The arms are made of hard rubber and therefore are unbreakable. These dolls embody all of the fine workmanship that Horsman Art Dolls have been given for the past seventy three years."

Peruggi is not known to have designed any later dolls for Horsman or any other toy company.

His long career also embraced portraiture, commercial illustration, and fine statuary, and perhaps his best known public work is a statue of the classical Italian poet, Dante Alighieri, in the Newark (New Jersey) Public Library.

He and his wife Susie lived in Fair Lawn, New Jersey, and they had two children, a daughter and a son. Long retired from sculpting, Ernesto Peruggi died there on June 14, 1957. He was 73.

The most prolific sculptor in the history of American dolls was Bernard Lipfert.

Longevity is one measure of his impact on the doll industry. In 1916, his facile fingers modeled Horsman's Gene Carr Kids, a set of characters from a popular newspaper comic strip. And, exactly 50 years later, he was responsible for the prototypes of Ideal's Baby Pebbles and Baby Bam-Bam, Hanna-Barbera's TV cartoon cuties.

Another measure would be his long list of hit dolls, including Shirley Temple, the whole Patsy family, Dy-dee Baby, and the Dionne Quints, to name but a few. In the 1930s and 1940s, Lipfert would design at least 80 percent of all the dolls produced in the United States.

Though at one time or another he worked for virtually every American doll company, Bernard Lipfert's long dollmaking career began in Germany, where he was born, Dec. 22, 1886. He received his art training as a youth in Thuringia, where four generations of his family had been toymakers before him, and where most of the world's dolls were made.

He worked first for the F. & W. Goebel porcelain factory and later for both Kestner and Armand Marseille. In 1912, at the age of 26, he emigrated to the United States, and Minneapolis, where he found work as an ornamental ironworker. One satisfied customer was Chicago's Marshall Field Co., for whom he crafted the intricate wrought work decorating the department store's landmark State Street clock.

The next year, 1913, Lipfert moved his family — wife, Elsie and their young son Max — to New York City. There he spotted an ad in the *New York World* seeking "a doll painter." He got the job and went to work for the Aetna Doll and Toy Co., Horsman's exclusive supplier of Can't Break 'Em composition dolls.

In time, his abilities caught the attention of Edward Horsman Jr., the company's artistic talent scout. Lipfert began sculpting doll heads. Years later, he would recall that his first effort earned him just $5 from Horsman.

After the Gene Carr Kids, there were other successful dolls, including Little Peterkin and, later, Tynie Baby, a Horsman response to the popular Bye-Lo-Baby. In the 1920s, Lipfert sculpted so many Horsman babies that he would later say that Effanbee's darling little imp, Patsy, had been his way of breaking free from years of designing nothing but baby dolls. Though Baby Dimples, in 1927, may have been Lipfert's last effort under his contract with Horsman, he was not publicly credited for its design.

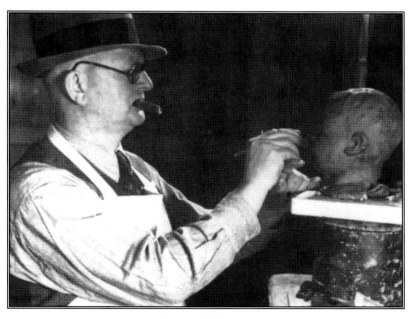

Bernard Lipfert.

By the mid-1920s, Bernard Lipfert had replaced Helen Trowbridge as Horsman's chief doll designer. But unlike Trowbridge, for whom doll designing was never the focal point of her life, Lipfert was ambitious and, frankly, needed the money to put bread on his family's table. He eventually concluded that he could do better working for many — and by the 1930s, it would be most — doll companies, rather than exclusively for Horsman.

The Horsman firm went to court to stop his freelance doll sculpting for its competitors. On March 25, 1927, an injunction request was heard by Justice John Ford in New York City's 1st District Supreme Court. Vehemently, Lipfert's lawyer argued that the company did not have exclusive rights to his client's talents. Lipfert was doing this outside work at home, in the evening, he said.

Equally vociferously, the company attorney complained bitterly that after all Horsman had done for Lipfert, now he was sculpting similar dolls for competing companies. In a dramatic gesture, the lawyer grabbed one of the look-alike dolls from the exhibit table. In doing so, however, he tipped it forward, and the doll let out a long, lingering protest: "Maaaaaaaaa!"

The wail broke the tension. The attorneys gawked. The courtroom spectators guffawed. Even the judge smiled, as he banged his gavel for order. That was enough for the day, he said, taking the injunction request under advisement. Later, the Justice Ford ruled against Horsman, saying the company did not have exclusive rights to

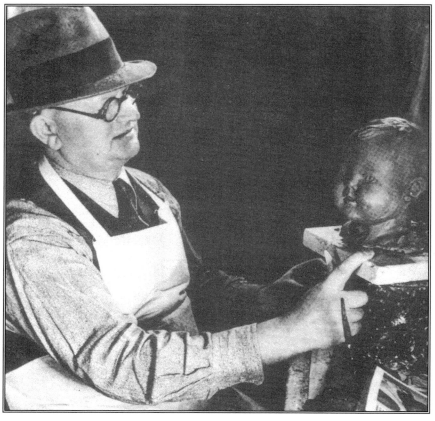

Bernard Lipfert, who in the 1930s modeled four out of every five composition dolls made in the U.S., began his 50-year career painting faces for Horsman dolls.

the sculptor's work. Lipfert was free to work for anyone.

By 1936, about 10 million American-made dolls were sold, and Lipfert designed most of them. *Fortune* magazine called him the "No. 1 designer of dolls' faces and dolls' figures for the whole industry."

In the basement of his Brooklyn home, the ruddy-faced, blue-eyed sculptor, wearing a pink rubber apron and a gray fedora — always the gray fedora — to cover his balding pate, created some of the most popular dolls of the day. His stubby fingers magically turned a lump of plasticene into Shirley Temple or Deanna Durbin or Sonja Henie.

The secret to his success, *Fortune* said, was *not* rendering perfect likenesses, but rather in "modeling heads that achieve the effect of a lifelike little doll without going so far as to suggest a doll-like little girl."

He seldom left his studio, *Fortune* reported. His clients, mostly, came to him.

"A doll maker will drop into the Brooklyn basement, talk design for a while, go on his way, and presently a new doll will appear, modeled by Herr Lipfert. If the doll shows any signs of selling, several more doll makers will drop around and in a little while, several similar and cheaper new dolls will appear, modeled by…Lipfert, who will charge the imitator not a great deal less than

the originator — anywhere from $50.00 to $500.00.

"At the same time…Lipfert will observe distinctions: heads for cheap dolls he will deliberately make to look cheap, and for originals that he thinks he may imitate, he will charge less."

On those occasions when a doll firm complained about a competitor's look-alike doll, Lipfert was happy to appear in court to explain just how close the imitation came to the original…or, if it was the competitor who paid his expert witness fee, how many little differences there really were. Later, Lipfert would maintain that no copyright was infringed if there was at least a 13 percent difference between two dolls. Just how such a difference could be so precisely measured he never explained.

Despite the 1927 break with Lipfert, the Horsman company in later years became one of the many doll manufacturers who sought his help in creating copycat models of the most popular dolls on the market. The Lipfert name, however, would never again appear on a Horsman copyright.

In the early 1940s, the sculptor, finally having become financially successful, moved from Brooklyn to a more spacious white colonial home in Westbury, Long Island. He set up his studio in a large second-floor sun porch. Here he continued to turn out doll models, year after year, typically working at a steady pace for eight or nine months, then taking off for a summer hiatus in the rural Adirondacks.

In the mid-1960s, age finally caught up with the prolific doll designer. His talented fingers stiffened with arthritis — he slowly "turned to plaster," his wife would say, just like the molds he made from his clay models.

On Sunday, Jan. 6, 1974, Bernard Lipfert, 87, died at his Long Island home.

Dolls of the Teens

"American Kids in Toyland," part of Horsman's 1911 line of unbreakable Art Dolls.

The years between 1911 and 1920 may fairly be called the "Golden Age" of Horsman dolls. Under the artistic direction of Edward I. Horsman Jr., and with the sculpting talents of Helen Fox Trowbridge, and to a lesser extent Laura Gardin, and an emerging Bernard Lipfert, the company brought out an amazing number of dolls, most of them — at least before WWI — with cloth bodies and Can't Break 'Em composition heads. After about 1916, most heads, and eventually bodies and limbs too, were made of a new wood fiber type composition called Adtocolite, an unfortunately difficult-to-pronounce contraction of <u>A</u>etna <u>D</u>oll and <u>TO</u>y <u>CO</u>., the maker of Horsman dolls.

Initially, Horsman introduced most dolls under the collective group name, American Kids in Toyland, a term that seemed to disappear from the firm's advertising after several years. Some of these dolls shared the same head type and can be specifically identified by name only when wearing their original outfits.

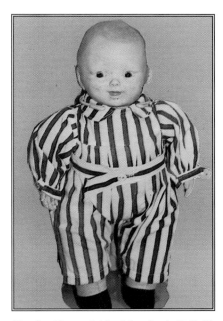

Early Boy: 11". Marked E.I.H. 1911. $200.00.

BABY BUTTERFLY — "Just as sweet as he looks," promised Horsman advertising in 1914. Baby Butterfly, representing the Japanese baby in the opera "Madame Butterfly," came perfumed with a well-known scented oil, Babcock's Corylopsis of Japan. The chubby, olive-skinned baby seemingly was modeled by Trowbridge from a life study drawing by a Japanese artist. The doll, which came in three sizes — the smallest, 13", the largest, life size — was dressed in a brilliant Japanese kimono, and its molded fingers could hold his parasol.

Horsman also sold an unnamed Oriental character doll as early as 1910. That doll had a round composition face with molded red turban, a squat, stuffed cloth body, upper arms and and straight legs.

Baby Butterfly.

Baby Butterfly: 13". Oriental baby, originally scented with a perfumed oil. Repainted, redressed. $250.00.

Baby Butterfly: 13". Restored. $250.00.

Baby Butterfly: 13". Doll has unmarked composition head with painted hair. $300.00. Courtesy Nelda Shelton.

Oriental: 11". Unidentified doll with molded turban has a cloth body, tagged Copyright 1910 // By E.I. Horsman. $400.00.

BAUERNKINDER — In 1914, Horsman introduced a group of dolls dressed as European peasant children. These cloth-body, composition head dolls, initially called Bauernkinder, clearly were influenced by German dolls of the time, and in particular, those of Kathe Kruse. The dolls had an olive complexion, described in the advertising as "sun-tanned." They came in two sizes, 14" and a larger model, perhaps 16" or 17" tall. With the start of WWI, things Teutonic became unpopular, so the German name, Bauernkinder disappeared from Horsman's catalog, and they were called, simply, peasant children.

Peasant Boy: 15". Before WWI, Horsman called these dolls German Bauernkinder. In 1915, the name was changed to foreign Art Peasant Children. $150.00.

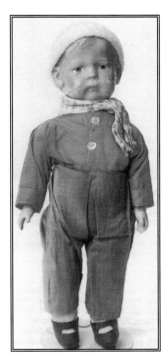

Bellhop.

BELLHOP — A jaunty lad in a bellman's uniform is one of the earlier Horsman character dolls, appearing only briefly in mid-1910 advertisements. He was said to be one of 40 "character models" with the patented Can't Break 'Em heads to be introduced that year.

BILLY BOY — Like many in the early series, Billy Boy came in two sizes, a regular 14" doll and a smaller Junior version, about 10". Billy Boy had the typical painted hair and eyes, which looked straight ahead. He wore a cotton tunic and shorts, an outfit described as a "Russian suit," with striped "Galatea" facings. He had composition Campbell Kid-type hands.

CAMP FIRE GIRL — This doll and her boy companion, **Boy Scout**, appeared in the Horsman American Kids in Toyland line about 1912. Though seemingly named for the outdoor youth organization for girls that was founded two years earlier, Camp Fire Girl looked more like a western cowgirl. She wore a "jaunty costume, all of brown khaki, fringed; a gaudy bandanna, broad sombrero hat and pistol belt with real pistol in the holster." Boy Scout also was dressed in a cowboy outfit, with fringed khaki trousers and matching shirt, and a broad sombrero. He also had a bandanna, holster, and pistol at his hip. His head was the same as used for several other dolls in the series, including Robbie Reefer and School Boy; hers is like the Jap Rose Kid girl.

Camp Fire Girl.

Boy Scout.

CANDY KID — Designed by Trowbridge in 1910, Candy Kid stayed in the company's line for about six years. He was described as "a jolly little chap with a two-year-old smile." The 14" doll had molded hair and painted features, a typical cork-stuffed cloth body, Campbell Kid type hands, and a romper outfit similar to those on the early Campbell Kids. It also came in a smaller size. In 1914, Candy Kid got a newly designed head, also sculpted by Trowbridge.

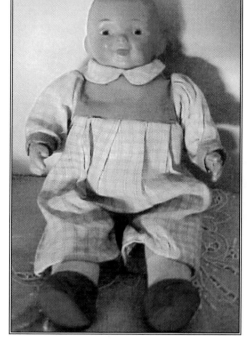

Candy Kid: 12". Doll dressed in original outfit. $300.00. Courtesy Linda Sonntage.

Big Candy Kid.

CARNIVAL BABY — A clown doll, appeared about the same time as Candy Kid and used the same head, although it was painted white, with dark patches, and was dressed as Pierrot, with a black and white sateen costume, wide ruff at the neck and cuffs, a pointed white felt hat, and white shoes. Also like Candy Kid, Carnival Baby got a newly designed face in 1914.

Carnival Baby: 11". All original except pompons missing from shoes. $200.00.

COTTON JOE — One of the original American Kids in Toyland, Cotton Joe, a black doll, came, like many of Horsman's Can't Break 'Em dolls of this era, in two sizes, 10" and 14". Initially, his face seems to have been copied from a French S.F.B.J. bisque head. He remained in the company's line for some half-dozen years, though his head mold did change about 1914. In addition to his brown-painted face, his stuffed body and arms were tan, but his legs were made of olive fabric. Cotton Joe was dressed in red flannel or striped shirt, brown or khaki pants and, in some versions, wore a broad brimmed straw hat. Other black dolls advertised included **Bingo**, in 1910, and during the 1914 – 1916 period, **Sambo**, in short tan pants and calf-length white stockings, red shirt with sailor collar, and a sun hat; and **Topsy**, with a hair bow stapled on her black molded hair.

Cotton Joe.

Bingo and Cotton Joe, standing.

Cotton Joe: 14". Early version, circa 1910. He got a newly sculpted head about 1914. $300.00.

Topsy: 16". Her boy counterpart was called Sambo. $350.00.

Gretel and Hans.

DAISY DIMPLE — This Trowbridge doll, whose composition head had its namesake dimples, molded bobbed hair in bangs, an open-closed mouth with teeth, and painted eyes, went on the market about 1911. In about 1914, Horsman revamped this doll, giving her a new and larger shoulder plate head and composition arms, shown off to good effect by sleeveless dresses. The 1911 version of Daisy Dimple took on various different persona, depending on the outfit. These included **Robbie Reefer**, a staple in the Horsman line for at least five years. Though his outfit changed a bit over the years, a constant element, and the reason for his nautical name, was the double-breasted sailor's reefer coat that he wore. **Gretchen**, also called Dutch Gretchen, was dressed in a Dutch cap and outfit, with striped stockings and felt shoes shaped like wooden clogs. She had a companion, **Hans,** or Dutch Hans. Horsman's early dolls also included a different Dutch pair called Gretel and Hans.

Happy Hiram wore a farmer's cotton shirt and blue or khaki overalls. **Prince Charlie,** a doll inspired by the eighteenth century pretender to the British throne, Charles Edward ("Bonny Prince Charlie"), dressed in a lace-trimmed black velvet court page outfit, with knickers, coat, and silk sash. **Jack Tar** wore a sailor suit with white or blue duck long trousers, a black tie, and buckle shoes.

Dutch Hans and Dutch Gretchen.

Dutch Gretchen: 15". Copy of a German face; molded flat top of her head. $250.00.

Campbell Kid Girl and Jack Tar, rear.

Jack Tar: 12". Early boy doll dressed in all original sailor outfit is believed to be Jack Tar from Horsman's American Kids in Toyland series. $300.00.

FAIRY — The success of the Campbell Kids led Horsman to seek other licensing arrangements with manufacturers with readily recognizable trademarks that could be reproduced as dolls. In 1911, such a contract would be negotiated with the N.K. Fairbanks Co. of Chicago, maker of Little Fairy Soap. Helen Trowbridge sculpted an especially endearing face that bore a striking resemblance to the illustration in the soap advertisements.

In 1914, Horsman introduced another doll licensed by a soapmaker. **Colgate Kiddie** was inspired by a character that appeared in Colgate & Co. advertisements. Little is known about this doll except that he was dressed in an all-white long romper outfit.

The earlier Fairy is much more familiar, a 12" doll with painted blue eyes, molded and painted golden curls, wearing a white cape and hood with a bunch of violets at her waist.

The same head mold was used for other dolls, including **Annette**, one of the American Kids in Toyland, dressed in a striped gingham dress and lawn pinafore. **Polly Prue** appeared in several different outfits, a patterned dress of lawn with a pink yoke and a dainty summer hat; and a white dress, wide collared striped coat, and large soft floppy hat.

Fairy.

Sold as a companion to sailor Jack Tar, **Nancy Lee** wore a two-piece, red-trimmed white duck middy dress. Her name may have been inspired by a popular novelty song of the era, "Pull for the Shore." Its lyrics tell of Nancy Lee, the daughter of a fisherman, who "dearly loved to float/ in her father's boat/ when some handsome man was there to hold her hand/ out across the sea they'd float and float/ 'til her Dad got sore/ then she'd hear a roar/ out across the water from the far-off shore/ Hey, Nancy, pull, pull, pull for the shore!"

Polly Prue.

Polly Prue: 13". $400.00.

FARMER BOY — Described as a merry "kid, all ready for haymaking," he was dressed in khaki overalls, a striped or checked cotton shirt, and a broad, trimmed straw hat. He could put his hands, farmer style, in the pockets of his overalls. Introduced about 1913, he came in regular and junior sizes.

FOOTBALL KID — Like the Campbell Kid Mascot, Football Kid wore khaki breeches and a sweater-type "blazer" with wide vertical stripes in assorted college colors. He came in regular and junior sizes.

GOLDEN JUBILEE — This doll was introduced in 1915 to mark the 50th anniversary of E.I. Horsman Co. She was dressed in what was described as "a tasteful costume of blue figured lawn, gathered in pleats and banded with lace insertion… neck is low cut and edged with lace…wide hair ribbon to match costume."

Jap Rose Kids.

JAP ROSE KIDS — Two Chicago-based soap manufacturers sold strongly competing brands during the early twentieth century. Fairbanks' Little Fairy hand soap was especially popular in the eastern U.S., while the James S. Kirk & Company's Jap Rose brand was widely sold on the West Coast. Horsman, having produced its successful Fairy doll, similarly negotiated a licensing agreement with the Kirk firm to market a pair of Jap Rose Kids.

The doll heads, sculpted by Trowbridge, a 14" girl and a boy, had painted brown almond eyes. She had bows in her hair; he had a "bowl-shaped" molded haircut. Advertising material described her kimono as pink, the boy's as blue, and both had an obi type sash. A different Oriental doll, dating to about 1912, was **Chinkee**, also known as Chin-Kie.

This doll, said to have been based on a Trowbridge illustration of a real Chinese child, was dressed in pink and green sateen blouse, black Oriental trousers, and black slippers.

Jap Rose Kids: 14". $400.00 each.

LITTLE SUNSHINE — Introduced in about 1913, this Trowbridge-designed doll had a cute face, painted blonde hair, and blue eyes. She wore a long coat-dress with distinctive large buckle on the skirt front and wide collar.

Little Sunshine: 14". Composition shoulder head, lower arms and legs. $350.00.

MASTER SAM — This patriotic doll and **Miss Sam,** his female counterpart, were known as Uncle Sam's Kids, and date to 1917 and World War I. About 15" tall, they were dressed appropriately and very distinctively in red, white and blue. They probably were imported from Japan and were made for Horsman by Taiyo Trading Co. Three other wartime dolls were **Middie**, a Navy recruit in a white sailor suit and high "puttee" boot coverings and white brimmed cap; **Rookie**, a young soldier wearing a khaki uniform, puttees, a brimmed hat, pistol and holster; and **Nurse**, with a mohair wig and what was described as an authentic Army nurse uniform. The last three dolls came in three sizes, 12½", 15", and 18½".

Miss Sam.

Master Sam: 15½". With girl companion Miss Sam, comprised a duo called Uncle Sam's Kids. $350.00.

Rookie: 16". Wartime doll from 1917. $250.00.

Miss Sam, Master Sam, Army Nurse, Middie, and Rookie.

Miss Mischief: 12". Composition copy of German bisque doll; molded flat top of head. $250.00.

MERRY MAX — The doll was one of a handful of characters sculpted by Laura Gardin in the 1912 – 1913 period. He is described as a laughing, bald-headed child. Other Gardin-designed dolls by Horsman are a short-haired **Eric** and **Peter Pan.**

MISS MISCHIEF — An early Trowbridge face with a particularly winning look, 12" Miss Mischief "can't make her eyes behave," Horsman's advertising said. She wore a blue and white dress. A very distinctive characteristic is the flat topped head beneath her blonde mohair wig.

Horsman also dubbed a number of other dolls Miss, including **Miss Muffet,** a cute girl wearing a blue coat with broad collar and cuffs, and a matching stylish hat. **Miss Nancy** wore a striped crepe dress with lace insertion and low-cut neck. She had a big silk hair ribbon. **Miss Molly** was dressed in spotless, frilly white, with lace yoke and white silk sash and hair bow. **Miss Janet,** who came in two sizes, also wore white, a dress of lawn, with yoke and lace trim, half hose, felt booties, and a hair bow.

OLIVER TWIST — He was one of several of Charles Dickens' characters who found their way into Horsman's line of composition head dolls. Oliver Twist made his appearance in 1914, one of the top of the line "Fine Dressed Dolls with Wigs and Glass Eyes." He wore what was termed an "Oliver Twist suit," a double-breasted white shirt with four buttons, modish short blue trousers, and a brimmed white hat. A 1918 Oliver Twist was somewhat taller, 16½", though not as expensively dressed. **Little Emily,** a character from Dickens' **David Copperfield,** was part of the same 1914 higher priced series, though a little larger than Oliver. She, too, had a mohair wig and glass eyes, and wore a pink and white dress, with a golden straw hat trimmed with roses and ribbons. By 1916, though still dressed in pink and white lawn, her outfit was not as elaborate, and she came without a hat.

Little Emily's childhood love, **David Copperfield,** appeared as a doll in Horsman's 1916 advertising, a chubby-looking boy dressed in blue silky jacket and cap, and white trousers piped with blue.

THE NAME "HORSMAN" ON A DOLL
Insures QUALITY, ORIGINALITY and DURABILITY
The Premier American-made Plaything.

The "Peterkins"
Trade Mark

Newly Designed

Send for
Catalogue
Just Issued

(Product Aetna Doll & Toy Co. Factory)
E. I. HORSMAN CO., Inc.
11-15 Union Square West
New York

The Peterkins.

PETERKIN — This doll, one of a series of unbreakable composition head, cloth body toddlers, was originally designed by Trowbridge in 1910, and sold continuously for at least a decade. Other, later versions of the doll were reintroduced in 1929 and continued to sell well into the 1930s. Peterkin's cherubic face made him seem like a distant cousin of the Campbell Kids. There were a number of different sizes and versions, including an early one with a jointed plush teddy bear-like body, and another with body and legs molded in one piece without hip jointing, like Kewpie.

In 1916, Peterkin was one of Horsman's first all-composition dolls, made of the new hot-pressed composition, Adtocolite. Peterkin became one of the most popular character dolls of the composition doll era. Trowbridge modeled the original Peterkin from life, although the inspiration for the smiling, dimpled, bald-headed doll seems to have been a nineteenth century children's story.

The series included toddlers such as **Tommy Peterkin, Betsy Peterkin, Willy Peterkin,** and others. There was **The Canton Kid**, a Far-East "cousin" of Peterkin wearing an Oriental dress, and, in 1915, **The Panama Kid**, "The boy who dug the Ditch, a charming little brown-skinned youngster from the land of the big (Panama) Canal." **Peterkin Fancy** was dressed only in a wide satin ribbon with a big bow.

A deluxe "super grade" series, with mohair wigs, glass eyes, and fancy outfits, included **Fifi Peterkin**, a sweet-faced French girl; **Pierrot Peterkin**, a carnival clown dressed in pink with black spots; and **Patty Peterkin**, lovable and naughty in her Sunday best dress and big silk ribbon.

During the same period, Horsman sold a smaller 11" **Baby Peterkin** as one of its Nature Baby series. A 13" **Baby Bubbles**, from 1915, had a Peterkin head, and was called "the jolliest, fattest elf of the year…bursting with health and good humor…dressed in his go-to-bed nightie." In 1918, a version called **Little Peterkin** was modeled by Bernard Lipfert. The 1929 series included Peterkin dressed as an Indian boy and a golf caddy.

Also introduced in 1915, **Dimples**, designed by Grace Drayton, looked more like the Campbell Kids, but was related to the Peterkin family. Like Tommy Peterkin, this 12" doll had a one-piece composition lower torso and non-jointed legs.

Peterkin: 12". All composition, jointed only at shoulders. $500.00. Courtesy McMasters Doll Auctions.

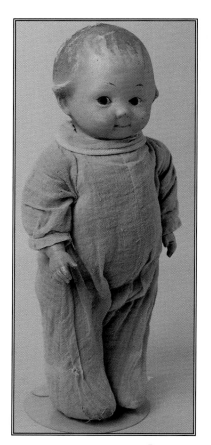

Peterkin: 13". $350.00.

Peterkin Kin: This family of dolls was introduced in 1915. From left: 11", Tommy Peterkin, $250.00; 12", all-composition Peterkin with shoulder joints only, $250.00; 11", unusual version with plush body, $350.00; 15", cloth-body version with compo forearms, $200.00; and 12", Dimples, with jointed arms but one-piece non-jointed lower body and legs, $150.00.

Tommy Peterkin: 11". $250.00.

Laughing Baby Peterkin.

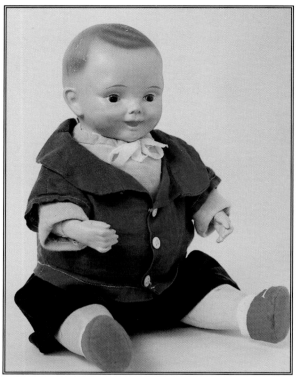

Baby Peterkin: 16". Hair not molded, but spray painted with distinctive stripes. Re-dressed. $200.00.

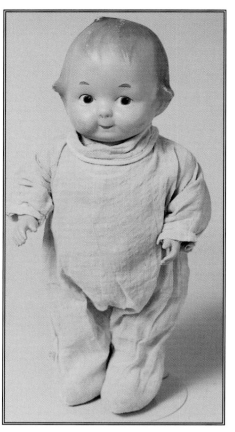

Baby Bubbles: 15". Marked E.I.H. © 1915, this jolly little elf had a Peterkin head. $350.00.

PHOEBE SNOW — The Lackawana Railroad trademark of a young woman dressed in spotless white became yet another Horsman doll with an advertising connection. The railroad, promoting a cleaner ride because of its hard-coal-burning locomotives, created the image of Phoebe Snow. Early in the twentieth century, the fictional Phoebe proclaimed in verse: "The miners know/ that to hard coal my fame I owe/ For my delight/ in awearing white/ is due alone to Anthracite." Appropriately, the doll was dressed like her namesake, in a gleaming white coat with lace collar and a frilly white hat.

RAGGEDY MAN — One of Horsman's most curious dolls, the Raggedy Man is a tribute to the memorable title character of James Whitcomb Riley's popular 1907 poem. The kindly Raggedy Man of Riley's verse was a farmhand who "worked fer Pa... the goodest man you ever saw!" Shortly after Riley's death in 1916, Horsman acquired licensing rights to use the character's identity for a doll from the poet's executor, Mrs. L.P. Tucker, believed to have been a niece. The sculptor who created the doll head, a nicely molded character face of an older man, is not known. The work does not appear to be Trowbridge's, but may be that of Laura Gardin who sculpted several other heads for Horsman about that time.

The Raggedy Man had a Can't Break 'Em head with a closed mouth, cloth body, well shaped hands, molded and painted brown eyes and hair. He was dressed in brown overalls, patched on one knee, shirt, jacket, and slouch hat. It was tagged, "The Raggedy Man/ Trademark/ Under License from L.P. Tucker/ Mfgd by E.I. Horsman."

The Raggedy Man

School Boy: 15". In original dress shirt, tie, and knickers. $250.00.

School Boy: 15".

SCHOOL BOY — This popular doll and his classmate, **School Girl,** were favorites soon after they entered the American Kids in Toyland line in 1911. They were still popular five years later. When introduced, School Boy was dressed in striped shirt and tie and dark knickers with white socks. School Girl, with a "cap" styled wig, wore a school frock and a large blue straw hat. Like several other dolls in the line, they got makeovers, including new faces, several years after their introduction. They also changed outfits. By 1914, she was advertised as wearing a "dainty lawn costume, with contrasting trimming and bright red ribbons at the yoke of her dress, and half length socks and buckled slippers." She had no hat, but wore a big bow in her hair.

By 1916, her outfit was a modish pink frock over a white shirtwaist, with white hat, short socks, and slippers. Her boy companion then was seen in corresponding pink shorts, white shirt with a broad collar, and a white brimless cap.

Sunbonnet Sal.

SUNBONNET SAL — A doll with this homespun name entered the Horsman line of unbreakable composition dolls in about 1912, where it remained for three or four years. Like many of the other early dolls, she came in standard and junior sizes. While the outfits varied somewhat, an apron or white overdress and a big poke bonnet tied with a bow at the chin seemed rather consistent elements of her outfit. Her face was similar to the Jap Rose girl, but Sunbonnet Sal had a mohair wig. A somewhat earlier Horsman model, dressed in sunbonnet and pinafore, was called **Sunbonnet Girl** and had a different face.

SUNSHINE — Trowbridge sculpted the face of this winsome little miss whose face and frock, Horsman advertising said, "combine to cast a ray of sunshine everywhere she goes." Copyrighted in 1913, the doll appeared in the F.A.O. Schwarz catalog that year, and in Horsman's sales brochures, in regular and junior sizes, the next. Her dress was white with a lace-trimmed close-fitting bonnet and a matching coat of ribbed fabric.

TOODLES — Another early Trowbridge-designed doll dating to 1910, Toodles received a newly designed face, also by Horsman's prolific woman sculptress, in 1914. The later design came in two sizes, about 10" and 13". He is described as wearing a patterned romper suit, then known as "smock and knickers," an English-style outfit for toddler-aged children which was just becoming popular in America. A 1916 version of the smaller **Toodles Junior** was advertised in an "Oliver Twist" type outfit of short pants and white shirt with wide cuffs matching the shorts.

Toodles, left, and Tootsie.

Tootsie: 14".

TOOTSIE — Helen Trowbridge designed Tootsie in 1911, with molded bobbed hair and bangs. She wore a rather elaborate outfit, resulting in a higher-than-usual selling price, of white lawn over a blue party dress, trimmed with blue ribbons.

Baby Dolls

Selling baby dolls that looked like real infants was the first step in Edward Horsman Jr.'s plan when he joined his father's firm as vice president. It was the reason he hired Trowbridge, and when she began designing such dolls, Horsman Jr. called them Nature Babies because, of course, they looked so natural. It was a collective name that would stay in the Horsman advertising vocabulary for a number of years. But because there still was demand for more traditional baby dolls, for a few years the company also sold some babies with the old-fashioned "dolly" face look.

Early Horsman dolls with Can't Break 'Em heads. From left, Little Sunshine, 14"; Little Baby Blossom, 10½"; Billy Boy, 15"; Sunshine Baby, 11"; and Sunbonnet Sue, 15".

Baby Premier.

NATURE BABIES undoubtedly are of most interest to collectors, though in most cases, today, it is difficult to distinguish between them.

They included **Baby Premier**, one of 20 new infant models introduced in 1913; **Baby Rosebud** came in sizes from 14½" to 26", wearing a French baby outfit of white with collar and cuffs of contrasting rose pink, and pink embroidery trim; **Baby Darling** seemed the same doll in a different outfit, lace-trimmed lawn dress, matching cape, and pink flannel coat, with booties; **Baby Beauty** was an upscale doll with mohair wig and a "French" outfit that included lots of lace, silk ribbons, and rosettes; **Baby Buster** was a 1911 model that, like many of the babies, came in a choice of short dress and hooded over-jacket or long gown, trimmed coat, and frilled cap.

DROWSY DICK was a doll different from the rest, with eyes half-shut. To complete the illusion of a nearly-sleeping child, he had a nodding head as well; **Our Baby,** which came in several styles and sizes, also had a more distinctive pensive expression, having been sculpted by Trowbridge and exhibited at the National Academy of Design in New York in 1913; **Baby Bobby** (sometimes, Baby Bobbie), was said to represent a younger, more serious looking brother of Baby Peterkins, with short molded hair that came to a point on the forehead.

Our Baby.

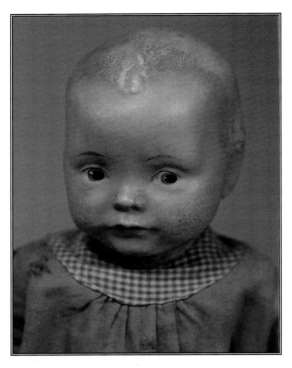

Baby Bobby.

Our Baby: 13". Early character baby, circa 1913. $250.00.

GOLD MEDAL BABY, another Nature Baby, copyrighted in 1911, was said to have been modeled after a real child, Adolphus Cody, who gained some short-lived national attention as the winner of a "beautiful baby" contest in Georgia. But since the contest had been held in 1909, and Adolphus now was a three-year-old, Trowbridge clearly needed another and younger model. She didn't have to look farther than her own infant son. Still, Horsman called the doll the Gold Medal Prize Baby.

Gold Medal Prize Baby had a Can't Break 'Em head and hands; the body and curved legs were stuffed with ground cork. He had painted hair and eyes, which looked straight ahead. The expression on the doll was described by the advertising copy writer as "suggesting delight at winning the prize." The doll came in five sizes, ranging from 10½" to 23".

In 1914, Horsman dropped "Prize" from the name, leaving Gold Medal Baby. It then became a line of baby dolls, which, in later years, included dressed and undressed styles, some with wigs and glass eyes. In 1914, following fashion termed the "French Craze for Colored Hair," certain styles came with red, yellow, blue or green wigs.

The later Gold Medal Babies included **Baby Blossom,** which came in sizes from 10½" to 30", and a so-called **Suck-A-Thumb Baby,** which came in sizes up to a whopping 33", and could not, in fact, simulate thumb sucking because of the design of its arm. (This doll should not be confused with a smaller and later Trowbridge-designed Suck-A-Thumb or a 1920s – 1930s Ideal doll with same name, modeled by Bernard Lipfert, both of which *could* suck their thumbs).

The Gold Medal name would be used by Horsman for various baby dolls for more than a half century.

Our Baby, left, and Baby Blossom from the 1914 Horsman catalog.

Gold Medal Baby.

Baby Blossom.

Gold Medal Prize Baby: 12". Re-dressed. $150.00.

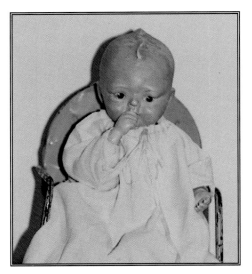

Suck-A-Thumb: 11". $250.00.

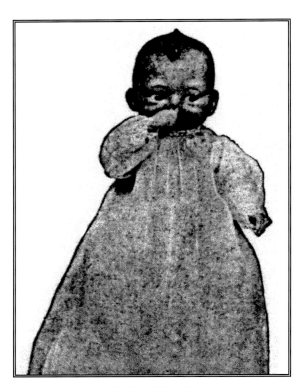

Suck-A-Thumb.

Wide Eyes: Three Horsman babies, circa 1912 – 1915, have painted, wide-eyed look: 10", lower left, Baby Blossom, $100.00; 12", right, name unknown; 19", rear, possibly Baby Premier, $250.00.

Early Baby: 18". Not all dolls in the Nature Baby series had character faces; some retained traditional "dolly" look. $250.00.

Dolly Face: 18". Marked E.I.H © 1915. Note that shoulder plate head is stitched to cloth body, typical of many early Horsman dolls. $150.00.

Christening Baby.

Baby: 17". Doll marked E.I.H. © 1915. Repainted, re-dressed. $150.00.

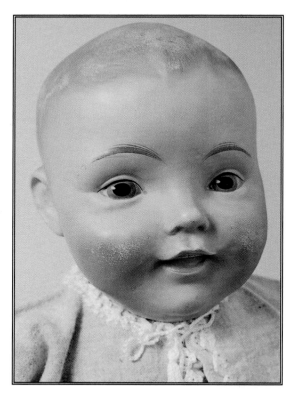

Character Baby: 23". Big, early baby with realistic character face. $350.00.

Late Dolly: 16". Dolly-face baby marked E.I.H. © A.D.Co., indicating it was made after the 1919 merger of Horsman and Aetna. $250.00.

Comic Characters

GENE CARR KIDS — These were a series of characters from artist Gene Carr's popular *New York World* newspaper comic strip, "Lady Bountiful." Horsman acquired the rights to produce these dolls in 1915, and commissioned Bernard Lipfert to model the cartoon faces. Over several years, seven character dolls appeared, although some of them may simply have been re-dressed and given different names.

They were 14" tall, had round faces and exaggerated features including a wide, smiling "watermelon" mouth. **Skinny** and **Blink** (and in 1916, a girl character named **Lizzy**) had eyes molded shut in a pronounced squint; **Mike**, **Jane**, and a black boy, **Snowball** (and **Smoke** who was also black and seemingly replaced Snowball in 1916) had big, round, wide-open eyes.

Blink: 14". One of the Gene Carr Kids. Re-dressed. $250.00.

Jane: 14". One of the Gene Carr Kids. Restored, re-dressed. $250.00.

Carnival Kid: 14". Blink, a Gene Carr Kid, as a Pierrot-type clown in white-face. Re-dressed. $200.00.

Blink's trademark was a vertically striped shirt, though in what seemed a cost control effort, in the second year, Smoke wore the same outfit, explained in advertising as Blink's old suit. Mike wore a turned-up hat and a vest; **Lizzy** was distinctively dressed in an ill-fitting, oversized outfit with wide horizontal stripes, referred to as "a thunder-and-lightning hand-me-down dress." Also, Blink and Mike came dressed in striped Pierrot-type clown outfits as the Carnival Kids, with Blink in orange and black, Mike in blue and white.

Encouraged by the success of the Gene Carr Kids, based on popular comic strip figures, Horsman looked to follow-up with another newspaper cartoon image, **Thomas Edison Jr.**, drawn by Fontaine Fox, better known today for his long-running Toonerville Trolley characters. In 1916, though, "Junior" was a "funny papers" hit with his adventures "in the interest of science." Like the Carr Kids, he probably was modeled by Bernard Lipfert.

Thomas Edison Jr.

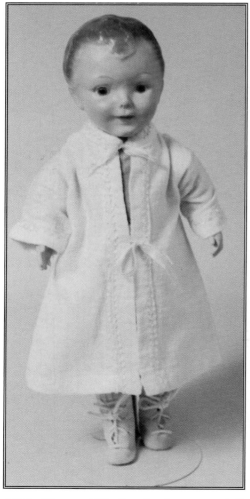

Little Nemo: 15". Comic character doll. $250.00.

An early licensed comic character, **Little Nemo**, was inspired by the *New York Herald*'s "Little Nemo in Slumberland" strip, drawn by Winsor McCay. The newspaper series began in 1905; Horsman's doll came in about 1911. He wore a striped pajama outfit with three buttons on the jacket.

LITTLE MARY MIX-UP entered Horsman's doll line in 1919, and remained through much of the next decade. This wistful little girl with the swept-back hair and perky bow was inspired by artist R.M. Brinkerhoff's cartoon strip in the *New York Evening World*. The cloth bodied composition doll came in 15" and 18" sizes, with molded hair or wig, painted or sleep eyes.

Little Mary Mix-Up: Original sewn tag identifying the doll and its maker, E.I. Horsman and Aetna Doll Co.

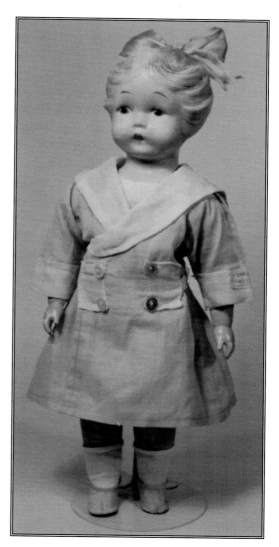

Little Mary Mix-Up: 15". Comic character doll. $350.00.

Other Dolls

BINKS and his sister, **Binney**, introduced in 1916, really were more pillowcases than dolls. Horsman trademarked them as **Hug-A-Bye** dolls for infants. Each had a stuffed cloth head at one end and feet at the other, with a pillow inserted into the armless torso. So soft and safe were they, "baby can take them to bed," Horsman's advertising said. Since the pillow could be removed, these dolls easily could be laundered, making them "strictly sanitary."

In 1914, Horsman introduced a series of dolls on wheels, or more accurately, doll pull toys. These included the **Irish Mail Kids**, the **Coaster Kids** and the **Cycle Kids**, sometimes known as the **Velocipede Kids**. They consisted of a Can't Break 'Em composition doll — boy, girl, clown or black child — attached to a toy vehicle, a tricycle, wagon or Irish Mail, a self-propelled handcar. Related to these were the **Crawling Kids**, a creeping doll infant on wheels.

Irish Mail Kids

"The Funniest Character-Artist in Toyland" was Horsman's description of **Heiney**, a hand puppet with a Can't Break 'Em composition head. He appeared in 1914 advertising as a comical male figure with an expressive face, wig, and "real" mustache. He wore a brimmed felt hat, velvet jacket, and brown pants, white shirt, and narrow tie. Heiney seems to have been based on a real vaudeville comedian, a German ethnic "artist" of the day.

Irish Mail Kid: 13" long. In 1914, Horsman introduced a series incorporating composition dolls and toy vehicles such as this self-propelled handcar called the Irish Mail. Doll has the same head as Our Baby. $750.00.

Fulper and **Nippon** bisque dolls represented a brief but serious effort to fill a gap in Horsman's extensive doll line. Though composition dolls increasingly were taking over, there was still a place in the American toy market for old-fashioned bisque dolls. With World War I, those German-made imports dwindled and disappeared.

Edward Horsman, Jr. had been hesitant to introduce substitutes, concerned that they would not match the quality of German bisque heads. It was not until 1917 that he took the first steps, contacting several prominent pottery companies.

One of these was the Haeger Pottery Company of Dundee, Illinois, near Chicago. At first, Haeger declined, saying that producing porcelain doll heads would be "too much trouble." Later, Haeger's chief ceramic engineer, German-born John Martin Stangl agreed to help Horsman.

Much experimentation led to a suitable slip mixture containing Florida china clay, feldspar, and flint. The Illinois company's kilns proved unsuitable for firing the bisque heads, however, and negotiations between Horsman and Haeger to construct a new plant for the production of doll heads fell through. Horsman turned to a ceramics factory closer to home, Fulper Pottery of Flemington, New Jersey, and persuaded Stangl to leave Haeger to oversee the project.

Fulper bisque head.

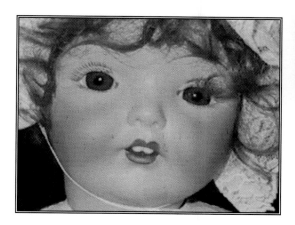

Fulper bisque: 20". This American-made doll was a joint project of Horsman and the Fulper Pottery Co. and is marked with both company names and the mold number, H-4. Composition body and limbs restored. $300.00. Courtesy Patsy Pritchard.

With the death of Horsman Jr. in the summer of 1918, Benjamin Goldenberg, Horsman vice-president, and Harold D. Bowie, company secretary, began working with Stangl to develop the bisque heads. On March 24, 1919, Stangl became Fulper's general manager and head of its new doll department.

Events moved swiftly. Goldenberg and Bowie supplied a number of German-made Armand Marseille heads from which copycat molds were made. In June 1919, Horsman introduced dolls in four sizes with Fulper-made bisque heads and its own Adtocolite composition bodies and limbs.

The heads were marked with J. Martin Stangl's initials, an entwined MS, and the name Fulper, spelled vertically, with Horsman incised across a circular symbol below it. The American-made heads also were marked with a mold number, such as H-1, H-4, 2-B, etc. In the summer of 1919, they appeared in toy trade magazine advertisements with chest ribbons proclaiming them, wishfully, "The World's Standard" and "The Perfect Bisque Doll."

At least one of Horsman's Fulper dolls was made from an American design. The Newark (New Jersey) Museum has in its collection a 1920 gift from the ceramics company and marked with the Fulper name, an 11" all-bisque Peterkin, originally modeled as a composition doll by Helen Trowbridge.

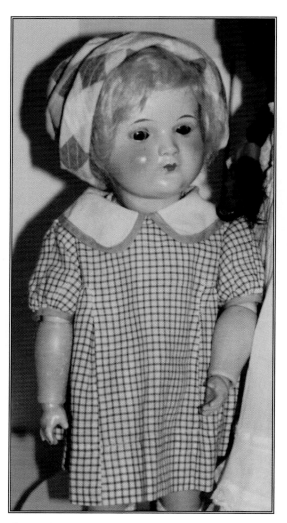

Ball-jointed: 16". Advertised in 1918, this doll has a socket head with sleep eyes and ball-jointed limbs. $300.00.

Nippon bisque: 17". After Horsman's American-made bisque project ended in a dispute with Fulper, it turned to Japan to supply bisque doll heads in 1920. This head is marked B-7 // Horsman // Nippon. Restored. $200.00. Courtesy Kathy Penn.

Fulper hired 15 new employees, local women, training them to paint facial features on the dolls. The most skillful of them, reportedly, was Stangl's sister-in-law, Pauline Case, who painted eyelashes.

With the porcelain factory able to manufacture substantially more bisque heads — 1,000 a day — than Horsman was prepared to accept, Fulper looked to other doll firms as customers. As usual, however, Horsman sought to control all production and objected to Fulper selling to its competitors. In the autumn of 1919, this dispute intensified. When it could not be resolved, the doll company went looking for another source of bisque heads.

Horsman turned to Japan. In October 1919, the *New York Times*, quoting a bulletin issued by the Japan Society, said a "New York concern" had contracted for half the output of a leading Tokyo toy factory, and that several of its "toy experts" were en route of Japan "to direct the manufacture of the goods." The report did not identify the rep-

resentatives or the U.S. company, but the timing of the deal suggests it may have been Horsman.

In 1920, Horsman ads no longer referred to its bisque dolls as American-made, suggesting the Fulper heads had been replaced by those of an unidentified Japanese porcelain factory. There were character baby dolls, dolly-face children, and toddler models. The heads looked very much like Fulper's since the same German prototypes were used for creating the molds.

These Japanese bisque heads are marked with a circular symbol, with the Horsman name incised horizontally, and the word Nippon sometimes misspelled, below. Above the Horsman name is a mold number, including B-6, B-7, B-9, etc., or No. 1, No. 2, No. 3, No. 4, No. 11, etc.

Horsman's attempt to market non-German bisque dolls was short-lived, however, and seemingly ended sometime in 1921.

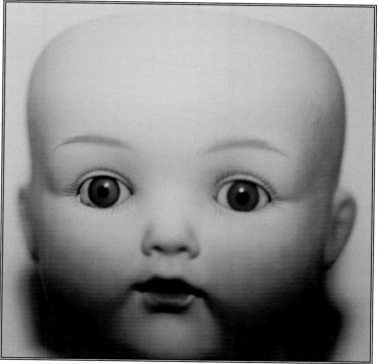

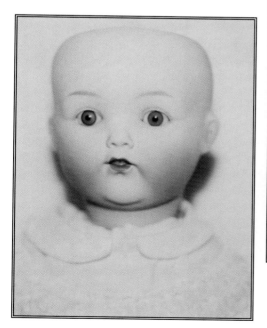

Horsman Nippon: 22". Japanese-made bisque head, 11½" circumference, marked No. 2 // Horsman // Nippon, on replacement baby body. $250.00. Courtesy Donna Mullet.

Horsman Era Ends

The death of Edward Horsman Jr. in 1918 robbed the company of much of its creative spark, but business went on, directed by his 75-year-old father, together with Goldenberg and long-time Horsman employees, Harold Bowie and William Ehrenfeld. Louis Wittenberg, called "the best toyman in the business," was chief salesman.

In 1919, the firm and its long-time doll supplier merged. E.I. Horsman and Aetna Doll Co., as the new company was known for the next three years, became exclusively a manufacturer and seller of dolls. All Horsman's old toy and novelty lines were dropped. The merged company had 350 employees and more than 60,000 square feet of manufacturing space in its doll factory on Lafayette Street in New York City. It also had separate facilities for making doll clothes and a paper box factory that turned out 5,000 doll boxes a day.

HORSMAN DOLLS

The Premier American Playthings

In our remarkable new line of Dressed "Art" Dolls with cork-stuffed bodies there are more than 250 varieties—in effect, a modish costume display never equalled in the doll world.

Early selection to secure the best of this assortment is advisable.

Product Aetna Doll & Toy Co. Factory

We urge promptly placed orders on the wonderful new

Horsman Full-Jointed Dolls and "Adtocolite" Jointed Baby-Dolls

Equal to the finest pre-war European Product

(Write us for full information)

E. I. Horsman Co. 15 Union Square (West) NEW YORK

Horsman's all-composition dolls made of a "hot-pressed" wood fiber material called Adtocolite were introduced in 1918.

In 1919, this building on Lafayette Street in New York City was the new factory of the merged E.I. Horsman and Aetna Doll Co.

The 1920s brought mama dolls — defined by their crier voices and cloth bodies with sewn-on "walking" legs — to great popularity after their introduction by Georgene "Madame Hendren" Averill. Like most other U.S. doll makers, Horsman followed suit in great numbers and with considerable sales success.

More distinctive Horsman dolls in the 1920s included Baby Horsman in 1923, Tynie Baby in 1924, the cherubic HEbee-SHEbee duo from 1926, and the perennial favorite Baby Dimples in 1927.

Charlie Chaplin and young Jackie Coogan starred in the 1921 silent film, "The Kid." Horsman's licensed Coogan doll became a popular success.

Advertising illustration from the 1920s showed SHEbee and one of Horsman's mama dolls.

Baby Dimples and Dolly Rosebud were added to Horsman's line of dolls in the 1920s.

Horsman produced a number of dolls based on comic strip characters, including Ella Cinders in 1926.

By the mid-1920s, Horsman Sr. was an octogenarian who had been in the business wars for 60 years. In the dog-eat-dog toy industry, successful companies such as Horsman continually were fighting off competition, some of it fair, some of it not so fair, from smaller "copycat" firms.

As early as 1910, the Horsman company published "warnings to the trade" in *Playthings* magazine. In 1911, an ad reproduced a letter from its lawyers, Briesen & Knauth, Counselors at Law, spelling out the copyright law and warning that competitors copying its Campbell Kid dolls would be sued for infringement. In a February 1916 advertisement, the company angrily announced:

"Horsman doll head models are copyrighted. Horsman doll names are trademarked. Various Horsman doll designs and doll devices are patented.

"Certain manufacturers, in defiance of law, have made reproductions of certain of our copyrighted heads and patented doll devices. WE HAVE ALREADY SUED the maker of one of these flagrant imitations and have secured an INJUNCTION

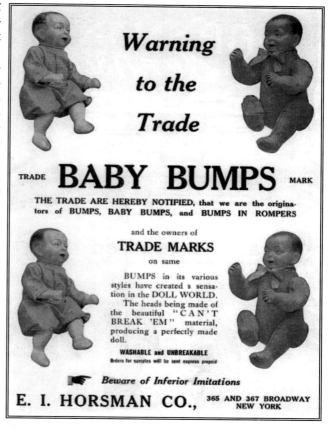

Horsman's attorneys warned violators that the company would sue those who infringed upon its patents.

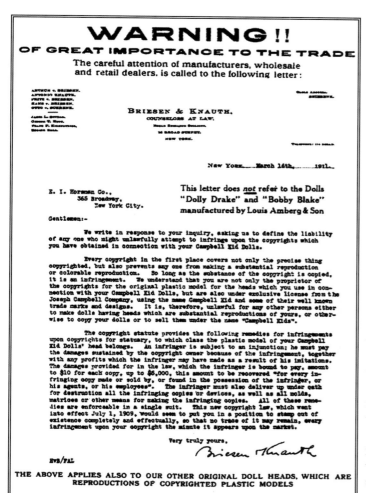

in the United States courts. We are now engaged in a suit against another.

"We will no longer tolerate such invasion of our rights, and we will PROTECT OUR RIGHTS AT WHATEVER COST!"

But it seemed a constant battle, and some cases that went to court were unsuccessful.

In 1922, the Horsman company sued Alfred Kaufman and Lawrence Cowen of Gem Toy Co., claiming copyright violations involving its Polly doll. The case was dismissed on a technicality because Horsman had failed to deposit two copies of its paperwork with the federal copyright office. Having learned a lesson, later that year the company renewed its copyright for its Baby Rosebud doll without that omission.

In an even more significant legal battle in 1926, Horsman sued Acme Toy Manufacturing Co. of New York for unauthorized copying of its Tynie Baby. Horsman lost that suit, however, when the court ruled that its traditional practice of marking dolls merely with the letters E.I.H. was insufficient identification. From that point, the company was more careful about identifying its dolls with the Horsman name, either with mold marks or with tags and labels.

Yet another lawsuit the following year would have an even greater impact on the entire doll industry. Horsman sought a court injunction to bar sculptor Bernard Lipfert from designing dolls for competitors. Again Horsman lost its case and Lipfert would go on in the decades ahead to design 80 percent of all American-made dolls, including such smash successes as Effanbee's Patsy series, Madame Alexander's Dionne Quints, and Ideal's Shirley Temple.

On May 7, 1927, scant weeks after the Lipfert lawsuit ended, Edward Imeson Horsman Sr., 83, died at his home at 157 West 57th Street, where, some years earlier, he had moved from Brooklyn. In his obituary, the *New York Times* called him "the dean of the toy business in the United States."

He was buried in the family plot in Green-Wood Cemetery in Brooklyn, beside his wife, Florence, who had died nearly two decades earlier. In the estate settlement, each of Horsman's daughters received a substantial inheritance. With little of their father's business acumen, however, they soon lost it through unwise spending and poor investments. The Horsman family had no further involvement with the company.

E.I. Horsman Sr.

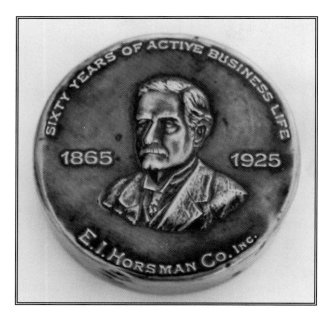

A rare 3″ diameter copper paperweight was given to retailers in 1925 to commemorate the 82-year-old company founder's 60 years of active business life.

Both E.I. Horsman Sr. and Jr. are buried in the family plot at Brooklyn's Green-Wood Cemetery.

Horsman company executives, Benjamin Goldenberg, above, and L.C. Wittenberg, right, died within days of each other in 1927.

After the death of Horsman Sr., his longtime associate, Benjamin Goldenberg replaced him as president of the doll company. But only 67 days later, Goldenberg also died, reportedly while undergoing surgery. He was only 59.

The obituary said, "his genius in designing and manufacturing artistic dolls found prompt recognition throughout the country and in foreign lands."

Goldenberg died on the day when Louis C. Wittenberg, the company's sales manager, 30-year veteran employee and the best-known doll salesman in the industry, was buried. In two months, E.I. Horsman Co. had lost its top leadership.

An era had ended!

Dolls of the Twenties

The decade of the 1920s was dominated by the mama doll, defined as one with a two-syllable voice crier that says "mama" and which has a cloth body with sewn swinging legs which can simulate walking. Georgene Averill of the Averill Manufacturing Co. created this type doll in 1918, but by the 1920s, Horsman and virtually every other doll manufacturer also were making mama dolls.

In 1923, trade sources indicated that eight of every 10 American dolls ordered by retailers were mama types. In the decade's latter years, some of this dominance would fade; jointed limbs would begin to replace the swing legs;

composition bodies would challenge the soft stuffed cloth torsos. But for decades to come, there would remain a healthy, steady market for dolls that cried "mama."

Though several American firms patented mama criers for dolls, one of the most successful — and the one adopted and used by Horsman throughout the 1920s — was invented by Burt Edward Lloyd of Woodcliff, New Jersey, and manufactured by his Lloyd Manufacturing Co., West New York, just across the Hudson River in New Jersey.

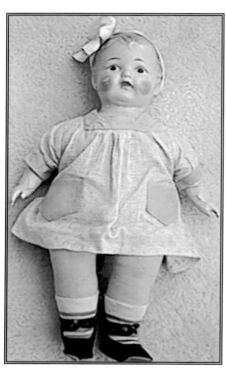

Swing Legs: 20″. Wide "bottom," cloth swing legs, and the mark on the back of the head — E.I.H. © A.D.Co. — date this doll to the very early 1920s. $60.00. Courtesy Katherine Manring.

Early Mama Doll: 20″. Shoulder head doll from about 1920 has disproportionately small arms. $85.00. Courtesy Carol and Andrea Kowerdovich.

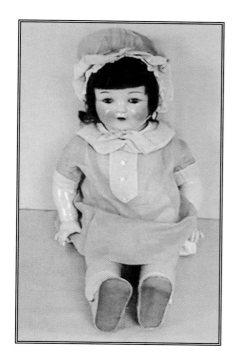

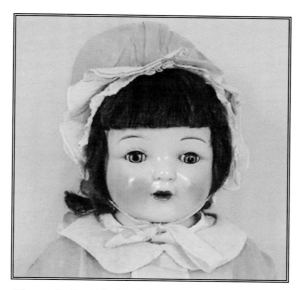

Mama Doll: 23". Cloth body 1920s mama doll with composition head, arms, and lower legs, tagged dress and matching bonnet, original socks and shoes. $395.00.
Courtesy Children's Planet.

Mama: 19". 1920s mama doll, left, $150.00, with 14" Sunny Orange Maid by Louis Amberg & Son. Courtesy McMasters Doll Auctions.

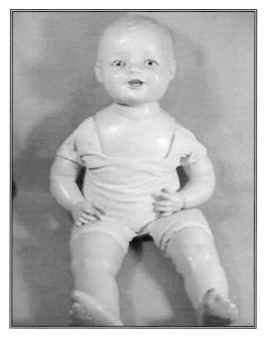
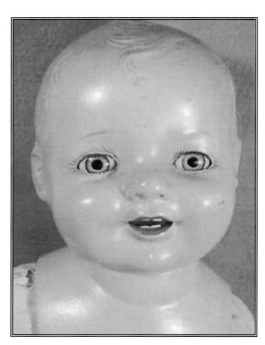

Mama Doll: 21". Mama doll has characteristic sewn cloth upper legs, but lower legs are composition, dating her to the middle or late 1920s. $175.00. Courtesy Donna Boulanger.

Mama Boy: 14". Shoulder head boy doll is marked E.I. © H.C. Horsman. He has composition gauntlet arms and sewn "mama"-type swing legs and wears his original toddler gown. $100.00. Courtesy Diane Chappell.

Mama Doll: 22". 1920s Mama doll with tin sleep eyes, open-closed mouth with teeth, marked E.I.H. Co. Inc. $150.00. Courtesy Cindy and Jim Adams.

Mama type: 23". Mid to late 1920s doll with composition head, arms, and legs, stuffed cloth body, original outfit, and brown mohair wig. $100.00. Courtesy Juanita Austin.

Well-dressed Boy: 17". Horsman cloth body boy doll from the 1920s wears original velvet outfit. $250.00. Courtesy Debbie Crume.

Horsman sold most of its mama dolls without specific identifications, but some were advertised by name. In 1928, it introduced **Dolly Rosebud**, a very popular mama type with composition hands and limbs, in sizes from 14" to 24" that would become popular. **Baby Rosebud** was a name Horsman used for bent-leg infants from as early as 1914. **Rosebud Babies** were mama types dating to the late 1920s. The Rosebud name on various types of dolls would remain in the company's catalog for decades.

Dolly Rosebud and Baby Dimples were advertised in the December 1928 issue of Child Life *magazine.*

Dolly Rosebud: 16". All-original doll from the late 1920s. $800.00. Courtesy Arlene Jensen.

Dolly Rosebud: 22". Doll in original outfit with cardboard hangtag, human hair wig. $500.00. Courtesy Dee Cermak.

Bluebird: 8". Peek-a-Boo is dressed as one of the Bluebird series of dolls from the early 1920s. $150.00.

Several distinctive Horsman lines from 1920 – 1923 included mama types as well as other kinds of dolls. Though they came in various sizes and styles, these groupings were marked by distinctive outfits. They included the **Bluebird** line, inspired by Belgian dramatist-philosopher Maurice Maeterlinck's popular play, and featuring a bird motif on their hooded capes; the **Red Riding Hood** line, more than 100 dolls dressed in gingham or lace, rompers or smocks; and the **Pinafore** line,

each of which wore a pinafore with bunnies in the decoration.

Though mama dolls with their sewn-on swing legs were said to be able to walk, in 1921 Horsman introduced a real **Walker Doll** with a walking mechanism inside the body. Its design was credited to company executive Harold Bowie. The Adtocolite all-composition walker had molded hair, was jointed at the neck, shoulders, and hips, and came dressed in romper, hat, socks, and strap shoes.

Babies

Baby dolls, with their bent legs, had always been important to Horsman. The 1920s saw the introduction of some of the doll maker's most memorable babies.

Among them was **Baby Horsman**, designed by sculptor Edith Hitchcock and introduced in 1923. Remarkably realistic, the doll may have been influenced by the success of Grace Storey Putnam's Bye-Lo Baby.

Baby Horsman had a composition head with molded hair, including a very distinctive curling forelock. The face appeared on heads with flange neck or shoulder plate, in doll sizes from 14" to 24".

Baby Horsman had a button nose and puckered lips, giving her a pensive baby look. Blue eyes looked straight ahead, with artistically painted "rays" on the irises and multi-stroke eyebrows. The cloth body was amply designed to sit easily; composition limbs were molded to realistic proportions; hands were dimpled like a baby's.

When a little girl put Baby Horsman to bed, Horsman advertised, the doll assumed a natural attitude. This was accomplished with loose stuffing at the joints, making its arms and legs somewhat floppy. The company promoted the doll as having the "soft cuddlesome feeling of a real baby."

Horsman introduced **Tynie Baby** in 1924, an infant also influenced by Bye-Lo Baby. Though usually seen with composition head and arms, Horsman also had 11", 13" and 16" bisque head versions, plus 6" and 9" all-bisque dolls made in Germany.

1924 was the second successful year for Baby Horsman, the company's competitive answer to the Bye-Lo Baby.

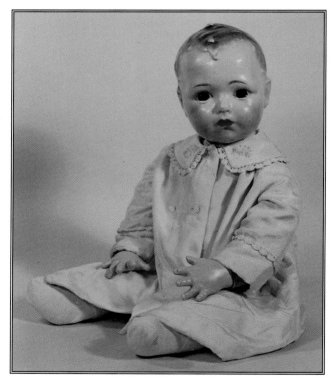

Baby Horsman: 24". Realistically modeled baby doll. $350.00.

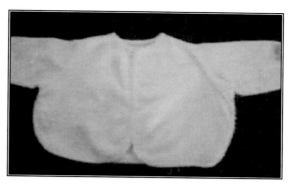

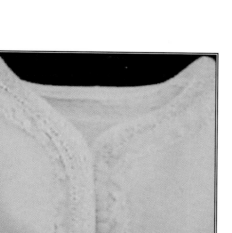

Baby Horsman: Tag sewn on arm of a kimono-like jacket worn by Baby Horsman.
Courtesy Karen Barnum.

Some composition Tynie Baby dolls had painted eyes; others came with the improved "celluloid-over-lithographed-tin" sleep eyes. The dolls had cloth bodies and bent limb legs. Some had full composition arms, others the shorter gauntlet composition arms. These dolls came in sizes ranging from 12" (sold individually or in sets of twins) to 21".

The earliest types are marked E.I. H. Co. 1924, but after Horsman lost its copyright violation lawsuit against Acme Toy Co. on a court ruling that it had failed to fully mark its dolls, later Tynie Babies were marked E.I.H. 1924 Horsman.

Baby Darling: 16". Cloth body composition doll in original dress tagged Baby Darling // Made by // Horsman. $250.00. Courtesy Myra Boyd.

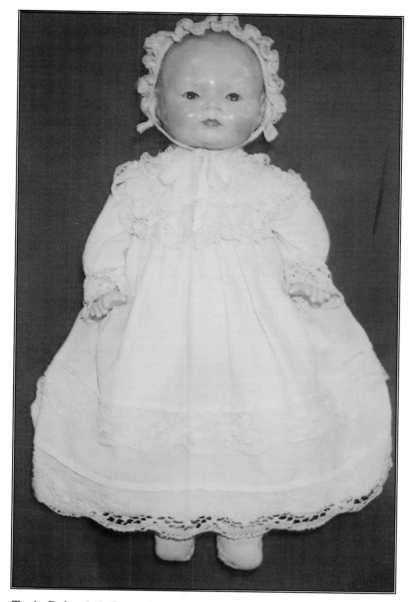

Tynie Baby: 21". Large baby is marked 1924 and E.I.H. Co. Inc. It has a composition head and full arms with cloth body and bent baby legs, sewn to the body. $400.00. Courtesy Stephanie Kornreich.

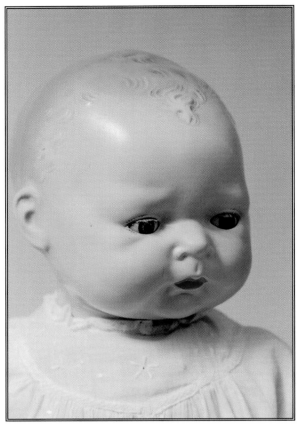

Tynie Baby: 21". $250.00.

Tynie Baby: 21". $200.00.

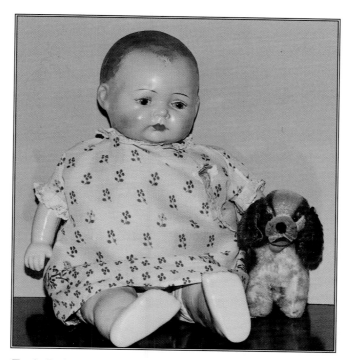

Tynie Baby: 19". Restored, in vintage outfit. $250.00. Courtesy Betty Houghtaling.

BABY DIMPLES, which first appeared in Horsman's line in 1927, was one of the most appealing baby dolls ever made, with its characteristic twin dimples in each cheek, and the crinkle laugh lines around its painted or celluloid sleep eyes. The cloth body, bent limb doll came in sizes from 16" to 22". In the larger sizes, the baby doll seems to have been sometimes advertised simply as **Dimples**. Also an all-composition, straight-legged toddler version was called simply **Dimples**. A so-called **Laughing Dimples** had an open-closed mouth with painted teeth.

There also was a celluloid head version of Baby Dimples. This head was made for Horsman by Rheinische Gummi under Celluloid Fabrik Co. It is marked Made in Germany on the back of the head, along with the German company's "turtle in a diamond" symbol, and E.I.H. Co. Inc. The head also is marked with the 1927 U.S. patent number 1545275 for the manufacturer's improved "wax-like" celluloid.

Baby Dimples: 14". $200.00.
Courtesy McMasters Doll Auctions.

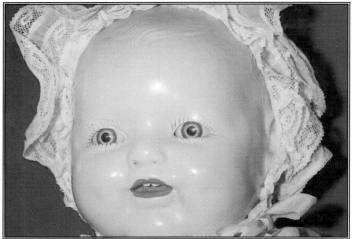

Baby Dimples: 18". Horsman's famous baby is dressed in all-original ensemble. $500.00. Courtesy Stephanie Kornreich.

Baby Dimples: 17½". Doll, marked E.I.H. Co. Inc., is from about 1927. Has full composition arms, attached with a spring, and inside-jointed cloth and composition legs. Restored. $80.00. Courtesy Diane Chappell.

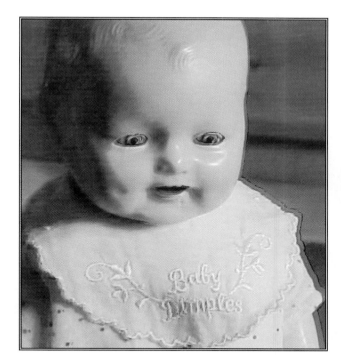

Baby Dimples: 13". A small version with original dotted dimity dress and bloomers, and oilcloth shoes. Seldom seen with embroidered name. $225.00.
Courtesy Pat Buccolo.

Baby Dimples: 22". Marked E.I.H. Co. Inc. $350.00.

Baby Dimples: 22". All-original baby from the late 1920s. $225.00. Courtesy Joan Rollins.

Toddler Dimples: 21". Straight-leg version of Baby Dimples. $250.00.

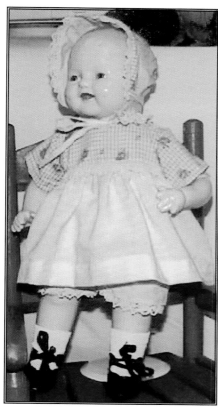

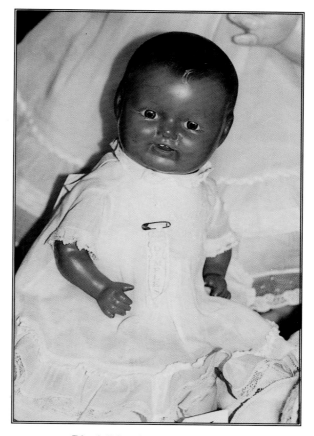

Dimples Toddler: 18". Dimples with cloth body, composition head and arms, and straight toddler legs. Repainted, redressed. Courtesy Jean Rollins.

Black Dimples: 13½". $400.00.

Creeping Dimples: 16". Unusual crawling doll from the late 1920s, similar to Creeping Baby by Sayco, but with a sleep-eyed Baby Dimples composition head, marked E.I.H. Co. Inc. Pulled by a ribbon tied beneath the arms, the doll's limbs move back and forth, simulating crawling. $175.00.

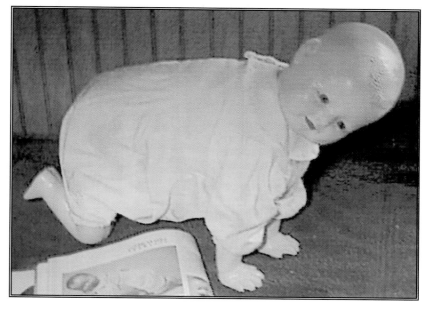

Cloth Dolls

Horsman continued to market its **Babyland Rag** cloth dolls into the 1920s, though by 1926 they had composition heads, arms, and legs, only vaguely reminiscent of their earlier versions.

Introduced in 1922, **Bye Bye Baby** was one of the last dolls Helen Trowbridge designed for Horsman. A cord was attached to both arms, and when it was pulled, the doll waved its arms and hands in what was described as a "lifelike manner imitating a baby's gesture."

Dating to 1923, **Dolly Jingles** was an oilcloth doll, about 20" tall, characterized by tinkling bells attached to the outfit.

In 1920, Horsman advertised its stylishly dressed **Manikin** French Models. From their long slim legs, clearly they were influenced by the then-popular boudoir dolls.

The **Wise Dolls** was a family of black cloth dolls sold by Horsman beginning in 1921. They included **Mammie Wise, Lizzy Wise, Baby Wise,** and **Miss Polly Wise.**

Ella Cinders.

Other Dolls

While Horsman seems not to have been as innovative as it had been during the previous decade under the guidance of E.I. Horsman Jr., the company did turn out a number of interesting dolls.

In **Ella Cinders**, Horsman again turned a popular comic strip character into an equally popular doll. Charlie Plum and Bill Conselman had taken the classic rags-to-riches Cinderella tale and inverted the heroine's name to create the widely read comic strip distributed by the Metropolitan News Service agency. Evidence suggests that Horsman had been interested in an Ella Cinders doll since 1925, but three years passed before she appeared on the market. In the meantime, Conselman had written the script for a movie about the plucky character. It was filmed in 1926, and starred actress Colleen Moore. When Horsman's Ella Cinders was released in 1928, the doll bore an uncanny resemblance to Moore. (Nearly a decade later, the actress would serve as inspiration for another well-known doll, Effanbee's Wee Patsy "Fairy Princess.")

Ella Cinders was an 18" doll with composition head, arms, and lower legs on a cloth body, although there also was an all-cloth version. She was as plain as her comic inspiration, advertised as "wide of eyes, freckled of face and human in expression." The composition head had painted straight black hair, center-parted, though a wigged version was advertised as well. She had a high forehead, freckles under her side-glancing wide-open blue eyes, and an open-closed mouth.

Ella came in a choice of four different outfits, each with a Peter Pan collar. One was a pink and white checked cotton dress, black sash and white apron; another featured a pink and black polka dot blouse and patched black skirt.

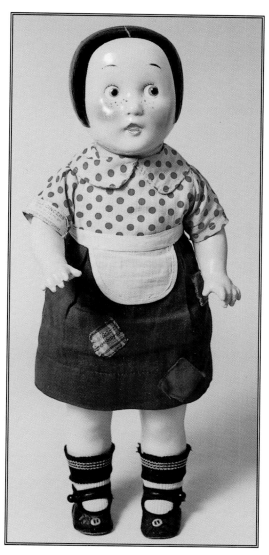

Ella Cinders: 18". All-original. $600.00.

Ella Cinders: 18". $650.00 Courtesy McMasters Doll Auctions.

In 1925, Horsman turned to another illustrator-cartoonist, Charles H. Twelvetrees for permission to produce two of his "Twelvetrees Kids" characters as both all-composition and all-bisque dolls. The artist's cartoon illustrations in the "Pictorial Review" and newspapers throughout the U.S. during the previous decade had endeared HEbee and SHEbee to a generation of youngsters. Horsman's dolls were equally well received.

The composition 10½" **HEbee** and **SHEbee** are seen more frequently than the German-made bisque versions. The basic dolls have bald composition heads, cute pink-cheeked faces, and molded, white painted undershirts. Their molded slippers are painted; his in blue, hers, pink, and have wire loops for inserting matching ribbon bows.

The composition dolls also were sold in a variety of outfits and were given special names. **Betty SHEbee** had a frilly dress and big hair bow. **Sunbonnet Sal SHEbee** came in gingham dress and bonnet. **Collegiate HEbee** wore a knit stocking cap and letter sweater with a big Y for Yale on the chest. **Pancho HEbee** was decked out in a colorfully trimmed serape and ten-gallon sombrero. The dolls also came dressed as bride and groom, Charleston and ballet dancers, sailors, bullfighters, and other characters.

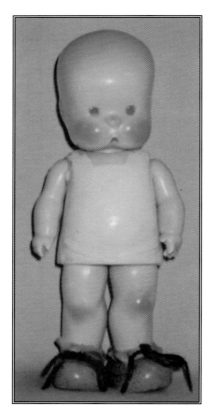

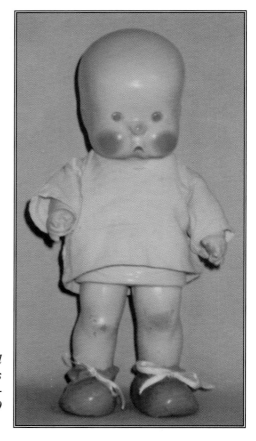

HEbee and SHEbee: 10½". He has a molded shirt, blue shoes with yarn ties; she wears original pink shirt over her molded garment, replaced pink ribbon ties. $400.00 each. Courtesy Dee Cermak.

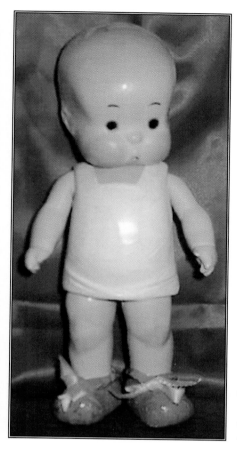

SHEbee: 8½". $150.00. Courtesy McMasters Doll Auctions.

HEbee: 10½". All-original with molded shift and booties. Repaired. $175. Courtesy Roy and Kathy Smith.

Collegiate HEbee.

Pancho HEbee.

Betty SHEbee.

Sunbonnet Sal SHEbee.

The 1921 release of the Charlie Chaplin film, "The Kid" made young Jackie Coogan an overnight star. Moving quickly, Horsman was licensed to produce a **Jackie Coogan Kid** doll, which it did, initially using an already existing head mold for the cloth-bodied composition doll. As soon as sculptress Helen Trowbridge could complete a new likeness of the boy actor with his familiar pageboy haircut, it replaced the generic dolly face mold. Jackie Coogan Kid came in two sizes, 13½" and 15½", and wore a turtleneck sweater, long pants, a checked cap with its visor cocked jauntily to the side, and a pinback button reading: HORSMAN // JACKIE // COOGAN // KID // PATENTED.

Jackie Coogan Kid: 14". $450.00.

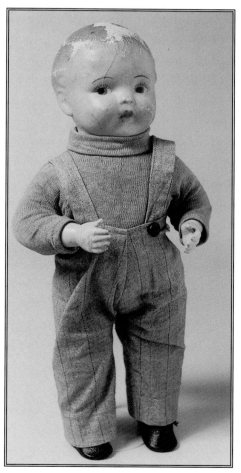

Jackie Coogan Kid: 14". Early version with dolly face. $450.00.

Jackie Coogan Kid: 14". All-original molded hair doll. $450.00. Courtesy Martha Sweeney.

Jackie Coogan Kid: 14". Unusual wigged version. $500.00. Courtesy Mary Evelyn Graf.

In 1929, Horsman brought back an old familiar name, **Peterkin**, though it was not the same all-composition doll that had been introduced in 1918, and marketed into the early 1920s. This new Peterkin family, which came in a wide range of outfits from rompers to Boy Scout and golf caddy uniforms, bore a strong resemblance to the Campbell Kids. This was no acci-dent. In 1928, Horsman lost its right to use the Campbell name. The soup company granted the exclusive license to the American Character Doll Co. which brought out its own version of the Campbell Kid, an all-composition doll marked A//Petite//Doll. Horsman's new Peterkin had a composition flange head and limbs with a cloth body. It was marked EIH © Inc.

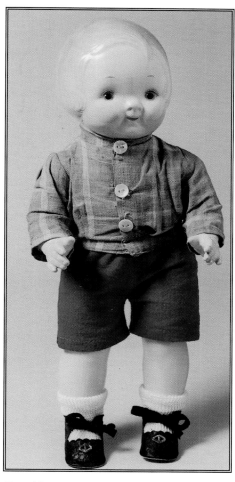

Peterkin: 13". Late 1920s version of this doll. All original except socks. $350.00.

Peterkin Girl: 14". This doll, marked E.I.H., has a cloth body, composition head, arms and legs and is from the 1920s. $250.00. Courtesy Elizabeth Surber.

Peterkin Scout: 13½". Late 1920s doll with composition head, arms, and legs, dressed in original Boy Scout uniform, including leather boots. $600.00. Courtesy Celia's and Susan's Dolls and Collectibles.

Black Peterkin: 13½". This girl, circa 1929, has cloth body, composition arms, legs, and head, marked E.I.H. Co. Horsman. $300.00. Courtesy Dorothy Bohlin.

*Peterkin Indian: 13". Late
1920s version. $300.00.*
Courtesy McMasters Doll Auctions.

Amberg Dolls

After Horsman acquired the composition doll lines of its former competitor, Louis Amberg & Son in 1930, it continued to make and sell some of Amberg's best-selling dolls for several years. One of the most popular of these was **Vanta Baby**, a composition head, bent limb infant with a mama crier, made in sizes from 14½" to 25". The doll was dressed in undergarments by Vanta, one of the best-known manufacturers of baby wear of its day. Horsman kept the old name but dressed the doll in its own outfits.

Horsman also manufactured the unique 14" **It** doll, which Amberg had named after Roarin' 20s movie "It Girl" Clara Bow. With its ball-jointed waist, it had been advertised as "the doll with a Body Twist all its own." Horsman dressed them in new outfits but for a time continued to make them with the old Amberg markings.

The Regal Years

With the deaths of E.I. Horsman Sr., and his two top associates in 1927, operation of the business was taken over by long-time Horsman executives William Ehrenfeld and Harold D. Bowie, each of whom had been with the company for 22 years. Quoted in trade publications, the two promised to carry on as before, designing and manufacturing high quality dolls.

E.I. Horsman Co. even expanded in 1930, when it acquired the composition doll line of one of its long-time competitors, Louis Amberg & Son. For a time, Horsman continued to manufacture many of that firm's composition dolls, still marked and sold under the familiar Amberg name.

However, the start of the Great Depression of the 1930s hit the Horsman firm hard. Other major doll makers brought out innovative new dolls — Effanbee's Patsy, Ideal's Shirley Temple, and Madame Alexander's Dionne Quints — which helped them weather the difficult times. Horsman did not, offering little that was new and different.

The Horsman management appeared to believe that the company's reputation for quality and value was enough. There is an almost plaintive tone to its early 1930s trade magazine ads that pled with retailers to remember Horsman's long tradition. Horsman quality, not price, is the key to maintaining a retail toy department's volume and reputation, the ads insisted. The argument fell on deaf ears, however, and the company's doll sales continued to slump.

Early radio advertising and a gold-tone medallion helped to sell a new version of Gold Medal Baby in 1930.

By 1932, E.I. Horsman Co. was in deep financial trouble, and in March, the firm reorganized as Horsman Corp. New capital was found, but the new company retained the same management and sales staff. A flurry of advertising promoted its own copycat versions of Effanbee's popular Patsy series and introduced a new baby doll, **Buttercup,** which initially had a composition head but within months became Horsman's first all-rubber doll.

Wishfully, Horsman's trade ads claimed that Buttercup's "mounting sales furnish conclusive proof that America's finest toy retailers are again appreciating the sales possibilities of high quality dolls," and still insisted that stores that stocked such merchandise would "add prestige and profit" to their doll departments.

The effort was too little and too late. Horsman Corp. was finished. In October 1933, it was purchased by the Regal Doll Manufacturing Co. of Trenton, New Jersey. It was incorporated as Horsman Dolls Inc., a Regal subsidiary. That month, a *Playthings* ad announced "The Two Greatest Lines of Dolls // Horsman Dolls // Regal Dolls."

"This year, especially," the advertisement continued, "you need the combination of Horsman and Regal Dolls.... Both in the Horsman Doll quality line and the Regal Dolls at popular prices we are ready with sales promotion ideas for volume sales, and our factory is prepared for big shipments and ready deliveries."

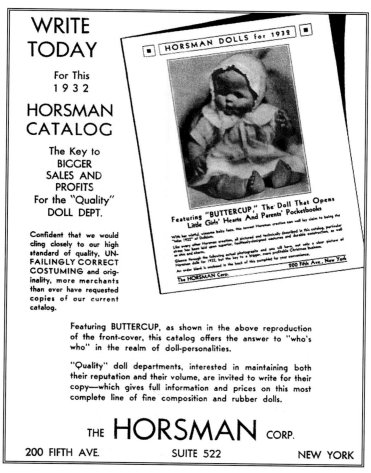

A reorganized but still financially troubled Horsman Corp. introduced Buttercup in 1932.

Regal's own early history is lost in the past. The first published reference to the company seems to have been in the February 1919 issue of *Playthings* magazine.

"The Regal Doll Manufacturing Co., Inc., formerly known as the German American Doll Company, is now located in its new and commodious quarters at 153 Green Street, New York."

Little is known of the German American Doll Co. From its name, it seems to have had it origins as an importer of German dolls sometime prior to World War I.

In its new factory, Regal produced "baby character joint limb dolls using an unbreakable composition." Its president was Soloman Apogi, its factory manager, S. Hubert.

In 1920, Regal, which had relocated to 50 West Houston St., New York City, was a smaller and less important doll maker than Horsman, Ideal or Amberg. An imitator rather than an innovator, it manufactured "character and novelty, full composition dolls with and without moving eyes…for the jobbing trade." Over the next decade, Regal moved its manufacturing plant several times, first to 61-63 Wooster Street in New York, then, in about 1929, to Jersey City, and finally, in 1931, to Trenton.

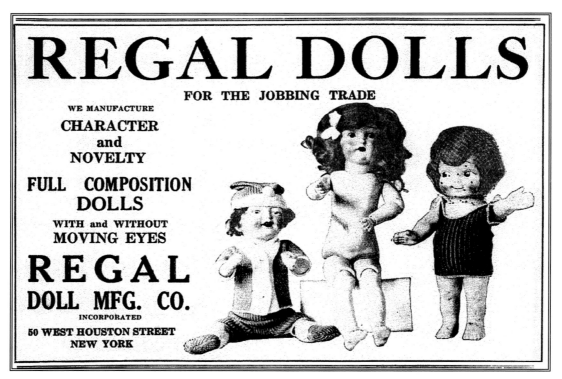

In the 1920s, Regal Doll Manufacturing Co. was an imitator rather than an innovator in the doll industry.

Regal seems to have been aiming higher. Its brand-new plant in Trenton was termed the nation's largest doll factory. It was selling a well-advertised and favorably received line of dolls called Kiddy-Pal. An accomplished sculptor, Ernesto Peruggi, was commissioned to model a remarkable likeness of America's hero of the hour, trans-Atlantic aviator Charles A. Lindberg, the prototype for Regal's impressive 33″ Our Lindy doll. The next step for the company was to acquire the venerable and prestigious Horsman name.

Horsman's manufacturing facilities in New York City were shut down and all production was shifted to the Trenton factory. Almost immediately, Regal had labor problems. Since 1932, Regal's production employees had been represented by a company union, the Trenton Regal Doll Workers Industrial Union. With the absorption of some of Horsman's production workers from New York who followed their jobs to Trenton, the American Federation of Labor set its sights on organizing Regal. After a year-long struggle, in June 1933, supporters of the existing union lost a representation vote to the new AFL Local 18247.

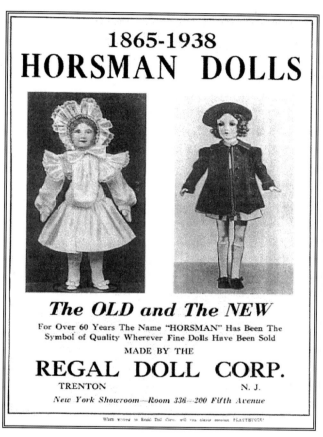

Recognizing its strongest brand name, the Regal Doll Corp. became Horsman Dolls, Inc. in 1940.

The doll firm sold dual product lines in the 1930s, but by the start of the next decade would drop the Regal name.

The AFL union signed a contract with Regal, represented by company treasurer Harry Friedman. Labor peace returned and despite some grumbling that the new union had succeeded in lowering rather than raising wages, it was clear that the Trenton workers fared much better than their counterparts at other doll companies back in New York City.

The Regal-Horsman connection sometimes seemed confused in the 1930s. Sometimes Regal's advertising appeared to suggest that it simply manufactured dolls for a quasi-independent Horsman Dolls, Inc. At other times, it treated Horsman as though it was only a higher quality premium line of Regal dolls. In 1935, Regal announced a new but short-lived pricing structure for the Horsman doll line that narrowed the price difference with those sold under the Regal brand.

During the decade, Regal-Horsman settled into a marketing approach that would be its bread-and-butter for a quarter-century. It concentrated on a small number of doll types, changing their clothes rather than their molds. Horsman dolls broke little new ground, except briefly in the late 1930s with exceptions such as Jo-Jo, the Whatsit dolls, and the Peruggi-designed teenage Sweetheart models.

The company sold dolls such as Babs, Sue, Jane, and Nan, to compete with Effanbee's Patsy family. Baby Buttercup, with her soft rubber body and trademarked Kant-break hard rubber head, became a drink 'n' wet doll to capitalize on the popularity of Dy-dee Baby. Bright Star challenged Ideal's hugely successful Shirley Temple. The line also included the company's own versions of the slimmer mama dolls that evolved in the 1930s.

But mostly, the Horsman name became synonymous with cute and cuddly baby dolls. Countless collectors who grew up in the 1930s or 1940s remember receiving a big, beautiful Horsman baby for Christmas!

The company focused its production on well-made dolls in a moderate price range, neither top-of-the-line nor dime store cheapies. Since this tended to price Horsman out of both Wanamaker's and Woolworth, it is not surprising that an important market became the mail order catalogs of Sears, Roebuck & Co. and Montgomery Ward where middle class America shopped.

In the late 1930s, Horsman made a number of dolls, especially baby dolls, exclusively for the catalog houses. Sears sometimes had its own designers create new dolls which then were farmed out to various companies — often but not always Horsman — to manufacture. Often these would have special names that Sears had copyrighted — Baby Darling, Baby Sunshine, Baby Marie, Miss Marie, 'Dorable, and others — that were used Christmas after Christmas regardless of which manufacturer had been contracted to make the dolls that year. But when the Trenton factory produced these dolls, the still prestigious Horsman name usually appeared somewhere in the Sears catalog copy or the dolls were recognizable by distinctive characteristics.

By the late 1930s, Harry Friedman had become head of the company, and there were structural changes in the business. Regal Doll Manufacturing Co. was reorganized as Regal Doll Corp. in March 1937, but the Regal brand name disappeared from its line of dolls. Horsman clearly was the dominant name, and, in April 1940, the corporation itself was renamed Horsman Dolls, Inc. About this time, another name, Larry Lipson, appeared among a list of company officials. By the 1950s, Lawrence Lipson would become Horsman's chief executive.

Through much of the 1930s and the war years, the company's emphasis on supplying mail order firms, and to some extent, producing dolls and doll parts for other toy makers, was reflected in Horsman's advertising in the trade magazines. The company apparently saw no need to promote specific dolls to old-line retailers, so most trade ads were small and generic, with little more than the Horsman name. Only rarely was there a larger ad showing a single unnamed baby doll.

HORSMAN DOLLS

FACTORY - TRENTON, N. J. • SHOWROOMS - 200 FIFTH AVE., NEW YORK, N.Y

During WWII, Horsman's advertising consisted of little more than the company name and an illustration of one of its typical, but no-name baby dolls.

Horsman geared up to meet the expected post-war demand for dolls. In a December 1945 *Playthings* ad, the company expressed its "hope that in 1946 it will be possible to satisfy your needs of America's best known and best loved dolls." Traditional composition head-cloth body baby dolls in greater numbers began pouring out of the 100,000 square foot, three-story brick factory in Trenton.

At the annual Toy Fair in March 1947, Horsman brought back an old favorite, an updated, all-composition version of the Campbell Kids. But composition was rapidly disappearing from the doll manufacturer's line-up.

Horsman geared up for post-WWII doll production.

Both the new soft vinyl and traditional composition dolls were advertised in 1947.

The 1947 toy exposition also saw the introduction of a brand new line of babies whose arms and legs — and in some cases, the entire doll — were made of a soft plastic called Vinylite.

Horsman technicians had been experimenting with vinyl since 1945, and two years later they were ready, long before their competition, to market such realistic, soft, lightweight washable dolls, guaranteed not to rot, crack or mildew. Later, a more flexible vinyl called Super-Flex was developed. Horsman dolls of softly stuffed vinyl were trademarked Fairy Skin. A hard plastic, Butyrate was developed for its "girl" dolls. The company promoted the fine molding and "lifelike tonality" of its flesh color. Doll wigs — and eventually "hair" implanted in soft vinyl heads — were made of Saran, a plastic filament like nylon, which could be washed, combed, and curled.

horsman
PROUDLY PRESENTS
Campbell's Kids

We're ready to greet you at the Fair
And help you get a good big share
Of the easy sales and the profits bright
For bringing children a new delight

The Campbell's Kids, familiar to every Amercian child and adult through being featured for 40 years in Campbell Soup advertising, have been reproduced with all their charm and whimsy by Horsman. You'll be delighted at their popularity and amazed at their low price.

horsman dolls, inc.
200 fifth avenue • new york 10, n. y.
factory: trenton, new jersey

In 1947, an old favorite, the Campbell Kids, returned to Horsman's doll line-up.

Horsman ads introduced dolls made of a soft plastic called Vinylite.

horsman

We are understandably proud because, only a few years after HORSMAN introduced vinyl plastic parts for dolls, this material has been adopted almost universally by the doll industry.

This general acknowledgment of the superiority of vinyl parts is, for HORSMAN, sufficient reward for the time, effort and expense entailed in developing the material and the process for using it.

The same pioneering spirit and constructive imagination which resulted in this revolutionary development has been applied to the creation of HORSMAN Dolls for 1950.

We consider them the most outstanding dolls we have yet produced . . . and cordially invite your early inspection.

america's best-known and best-loved dolls

horsman dolls, inc.

200 fifth avenue   new york 10, n. y.

factory: trenton, new jersey   telephone OR 5-172[

dolls

Late 1949 trade publication ad proudly explains that Horsman was the first company to introduce soft vinyl plastic to the doll industry.

In 1950, as Horsman marked its 85th birthday and the end of the composition era it had begun four decades earlier, the factory produced one million plastic dolls, 12" to 26" tall, sometimes as many as 12,000 a day during the peak production months of August and September.

Thousands of doll heads awaiting face painting in Horsman's Trenton factory in about 1950.

Horsman employees style doll wigs at the Trenton plant, circa 1950.

Dolls awaiting shipment from the Trenton Horsman factory about 1949.

Ramon B. Fisch, the company's vice president of operations, said Horsman's aim was still to make and sell a "People's Doll, a fine doll at a moderate price." Ninety-five percent of Horsman's output was baby dolls, which were sold across the country and around the world, from South America to Hong Kong.

The other 5 percent were what Fisch somewhat scornfully described as "trick" dolls, the sort that walk, talk, sing, whistle or dance! Though competitors increasingly were mass-marketing such "trick" dolls on TV, Horsman, by and large, avoided the genre.

The company employed about 800 workers, many of whom lived in the neighborhood of the factory that covered a solid block bounded by Trenton's Adeline, Chestnut, Grand, and Elm streets.

In Trenton they made dolls the way Detroit made cars, on an assembly line, with separate departments supplying the heads, bodies, arms, and legs. Thirty-five women artists painted the features; there were 60 to 70 wigmakers, a particularly demanding job requiring formal apprenticeship training.

The dressmaking department had 250 to 300 women operating sewing machines. To keep those machines constantly humming, a crew of men used electric knives to cut out the fabric pieces, 216 thicknesses of cloth at a time.

From start to finish — and production manager George Zurio estimated it took about three days to make a doll and package it — Horsman employees did it all. The company even had its own box factory, turning out doll boxes of all sizes.

It was all quite remarkable. E.I. Horsman Sr. would have been proud.

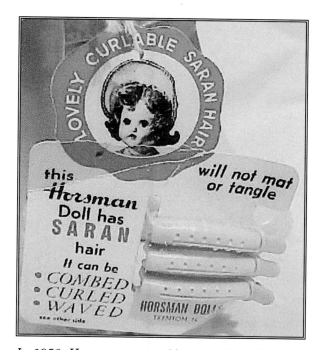

In 1950, Horsman was making everything from doll boxes to mohair wigs. The next year it introduced another innovation, Saran wigs that could be washed, combed, and styled.

Dolls of the Thirties & Forties

Even before Regal purchased Horsman in 1933, things had begun to change. By the early 1930s, its reputation for innovation had begun to slip. When, for example, competitor Effanbee struck gold with its new and growing family of Patsy dolls, Horsman could only copycat.

After Regal's acquisition, Horsman originality suffered further. While a solid player, Regal was more a follower than a leader. In the 1920s, generally it had been willing to let the more progressive companies takes the risk of introducing innovative new dolls. Regal found its place in the industry's "second tier" of doll manufacturers, turning out its own similar — but less expensive — versions of already popular dolls.

While continuing to market its two brands, the cheaper Regal line and the somewhat upscale Horsman dolls, through retail stores, the doll manufacturer increasingly became a supplier for the large mail order houses, Sears, Roebuck & Co. and Montgomery Ward. Dolls identified as made by Horsman frequently are found in their Christmas catalogs throughout the 1930s and 1940s.

Although through the 1930s Horsman was simply a line of dolls made by Regal, for the sake of clarity, we will refer to these dolls as though Horsman had remained a separate manufacturing entity. In the early 1940s, this became reality when the Regal corporate identity was abandoned and the Horsman company name was reborn.

Beginning in the 1930s, a new corporate policy began to evolve, one that would continue for two decades and beyond. It was a policy of limiting its doll line to a relatively few types, but concentrating — up to 80 percent of its production in some years — on pretty baby dolls.

Horsman dolls would come in many new and varied outfits over the years, but the dolls themselves would change only slowly. Horsman's reputation for well-made dolls would continue, but the firm would price them for a middle-class, middle-American market.

It was a policy that Horsman would articulate and reaffirm in 1950, when its then vice president of operations, Ramon B. Fisch, said, "We make a fine doll at a moderate price… a 'People's Doll.'"

Look-Alikes

Horsman's first attempt to compete with Effanbee's popular Patsy came in 1930, with the acquisition of the Amberg name and composition doll line. The firm simply redressed Amberg's 14", jointed-waist "It" girl, and called her **Peggy**. Next came a 12" version of the same all-composition doll, which seems to have been called **Peggy Jr.**, followed by a 20" cloth body **Peggy Ann**, with a swivel head on a shoulder plate.

Horsman ad from 1930. Note that Peggy, a doll acquired when Horsman purchased the Amberg composition line that year, is advertised in addition to Dolly Rosebud and Baby Dimples.

Peggy family: From left, Peggy, 14", is Amberg's jointed-waist It girl in an updated outfit, $250.00; Peggy Ann, 20", is the larger version, $350.00; and Peggy Jr., 12", is the little sister, $350.00.

But this series, intended to compete with similarly sized Patsy, Patsykins, and Patsy Ann, respectively, did not fare well, probably because they really didn't look enough like the impish Effanbee dolls.

In 1931, they were replaced with four new look-alikes that more closely resembled the Patsy family. They were **Babs**, 12"; **Sue**, 14"; **Jane**, 17½", and **Nan**, 20". Sue had the same Amberg-type twist-waist body as her predecessors, Peggy and It. One version, called **Skating Sue,** came with roller skates.

By 1934, these four were available with molded hair, with wigs of mohair curled into fine ringlets, or human hair in long curls. Babs had metal sleep eyes; the larger dolls had glassene eyes.

In addition, in 1931, Horsman is said to have also produced several dolls exclusively for Sears, Roebuck & Co. which somewhat resembled Patsy and were sold under Sears' own trademarked names, **Dainty Dorothy** and **Sally**.

Patsy Look-Alikes: In 1931, Horsman introduced four dolls to compete with Effanbee's Patsy family. Rear, from left, 20", Nan, $300.00, and 17½", Jane, $250.00. Front, from left, 14", Sue, in white and black versions, $200.00 and $250.00, and 12", Babs, $200.00.

Rubber baby dolls began appearing in the 1930s. **Buttercup** was Horsman's answer to Lamkin by Effanbee. At first Buttercup had a composition head, rubber body and limbs, outstretched arms, and curved baby legs. Soon, though, hard rubber heads replaced composition, and the advertising would tout an all-rubber doll. In various sizes, the doll also was called **Wee Buttercup**, **Tiny Buttercup**, **Little Buttercup,** and **Baby Buttercup**. After Effanbee introduced Dy-Dee Baby, its initially controversial drink 'n' wet doll, in 1934, Horsman followed suit, making Baby Buttercup a fully jointed, all-rubber sleep eye doll with its own drink-wet mechanism.

Nan and Jane.

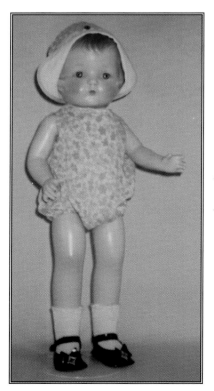

Jane: 17½". Horsman's answer to Effanbee's Patsy Joan. Re-dressed. $250.00.
Courtesy Dee Cermak.

Buttercup was part of Horsman's regular line, not manufactured exclusively for Sears, Roebuck & Co., however this doll was featured in Sears 1933 Christmas catalog.

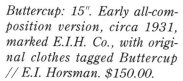

Buttercup: 15". Early all-composition version, circa 1931, marked E.I.H. Co., with original clothes tagged Buttercup // E.I. Horsman. $150.00.

In the mid to late 1930s, the extreme popularity of Ideal's celebrity doll, Shirley Temple, led many U.S. doll makers, including Horsman, to bring out their own copy-cat versions. Because only Ideal was licensed to use the name of the young motion picture star, the others makers adopted different names for their dolls. For Horsman, it was **Bright Star**, who stood in for Shirley Temple. She was an all-composition, fully-jointed doll with second and third fingers molded together, a mohair wig, sleep eyes, and open mouth with teeth.

She came in various sizes, from about 12" to 20". While hardly a "dead ringer" for Ideal's dimpled cutie, Bright Star, a very pretty doll in her own right, could pass for Shirley, particularly when dressed in outfits that looked a lot like the movie originals.

Bright Star: 11". A Horsman alternative to Ideal's Shirley Temple. $400.00. Courtesy Arlene Jensen.

Bright Star: 20". A Shirley Temple look-alike, left, $350.00, with Giggles by Cameo Doll Co. Courtesy McMasters Doll Auctions.

Bright Star: 13". $250.00.

Cardboard hang tag from Horsman's Bright Star composition doll.

Similarly dressed and with a curly wig, Horsman also sold its Babs/Sue/Jane/Nan line as a competitor to Shirley Temple. Another copycat was called, simply, **Shirley Little Colonel**. She had mohair wig, similar dimpled face, sleep eyes, open mouth with teeth, and a lavender version of the Little Colonel outfit.

A 1934 Horsman catalog shows **Miss Charming**, a swivel-head, shoulder plate composition doll with cloth body, in five sizes, 16" to 25", with Shirley-like curls and outfit. The cheaper Regal line dressed one of its Kiddie Pal dolls to look like Shirley as well.

Bright Star later took on other roles too. In whichever outfits matched the then-current doll competition, Horsman matched her against the likes of Judy Garland, Deanna Durbin, Little Lady majorette, and others. Bright Star, in various sizes and dress, remained a fixture in Horsman's composition line-up throughout the 1940s, and in the early 1950s as a hard plastic doll with open mouth and Saran hair.

In 1937, with the release of Walt Disney's animated film, Knickerbocker and Madame Alexander brought out licensed Snow White dolls. Horsman responded with its own doll, 19" and all-composition, with green sleep eyes, open mouth with four teeth, and felt tongue. Though she closely resembled Snow White — beige skirt trimmed in red rickrack, red velvet top and outer cape, black mohair wig with ribbon and pins — as an unlicensed copycat, Horsman did not identify her as the Disney heroine.

Ice Skater: 13". All-composition Gold Medal toddler doll with a "crown" of blonde mohair braids; Horsman's answer to Madame Alexander's licensed Sonja Henie. $400.00. Courtesy Geri Perlstein.

In the late 1930s, Effanbee's American Children, designed by sculptress Dewees Cochran, brought a new level of artistic modeling to doll making. Horsman's answer to this challenge was to commission well-known sculptor Ernesto Peruggi to model in 1938 the prototype for its **Sweetheart**, described as "a true reproduction of girls between the ages of ten and sixteen." Slim and tall, these were truly lovely dolls, all-composition except for their hard rubber arms with delicately molded fingers. Sweetheart, in nominally 21", 24", and 28" sizes, was dressed in the latest teen style. "These dolls embody all of the fine workmanship that Horsman Art Dolls have been giving for the past seventy three years," the company advertised.

Sweetheart: 28" and 24". $850.00 and $700.00.

Sweetheart: 28". All-original doll wearing the outfit shown in the 1938 John Plain mail order catalog. $800.00. Courtesy Diane Dustir.

Sweetheart; 21". Smallest of Horsman's artistic teenage series. $700.00. Courtesy Willy Ginaven.

24-Inch Horsman "Sweetheart Doll." Just like a growing girl. Fully jointed composition body, legs and swivel head. "Kantbreak" hard rubber arms. Moving glass eyes and eyelashes. Open mouth showing teeth and tongue. Fine quality sewed mohair wigs. Dressed in assorted dresses such as young girls wear. Fine quality cloth coats with curled plush trimmings. Combination rayon silk petticoat and bloomer, shoes and stockings. Hats to match. Each in box.

No. 36N172   Each $8.40

28-Inch Horsman "Sweetheart Doll." Self-standing growing girl type. All composition fully jointed body, arms, legs and swivel head. Arms made of unbreakable hard rubber. Moving glass eyes and eyelashes. Open mouth showing teeth and tongue. Fine mohair wig. Assorted dresses and cloth coats. Matching hats. Each in box.

No. 36N173   Each $9.80

Horsman's teenage Sweetheart dolls, 24" and 28", were advertised in the John Plain 1939 catalog.

Mystery has surrounded the so-called **Jeanette Mac-Donald** doll, a specially dressed and coiffed Horsman Sweetheart doll. Even information from famed doll designer Mollye Goldman, recounted in her twilight years, adds as much confusion as explanation.

The full story may never be known, but a plausible version of Goldman's tale is that in 1938, a buyer for a Philadelphia department store, Wanamaker's, struck by a happy coincidence, the release of Horsman's teenage doll, Sweetheart and the popular success of the musical film, "Sweethearts," contacted Mollye Goldman. Design a doll to represent the movie's musical leading lady, Jeanette MacDonald, he asked.

The buyer — his name comes to us as John McDonald — supplied a doll, an off-the-shelf Horsman Sweet-heart which Mollye custom dressed. The original doll was presented to America's singing sweetheart during a Philadelphia appearance, Goldman claimed, four decades later. Favorable publicity generated by this stunt prompted Wanamaker's to commission Goldman to produce about 50 more Jeanette MacDonald dolls that were sold by the Philadelphia department store.

A few of them seem to have survived, making this a very rare doll!

Horsman never advertised a Jeanette MacDonald; there was no national advertising campaign. If there were local Wanamaker ads for the doll in the Philadelphia newspapers, we have not found them.

Jeanette MacDonald: 28″. Sweetheart said to have been dressed as the musical film actress by Mollye Goldman on special order from Wanamaker's department store in Philadelphia. $1,500.00. Courtesy Diane Dustir.

Familiar Names

Successful names such as Bright Star remained in the Horsman doll line for years, even decades. The **Gold Medal Baby** name was revived in 1931 in a curious joint effort by the E.I. Horsman Co. and the Averill Co. Inc. This new baby doll was sold under both the Horsman and Madame Hendren labels, wearing a goldtone medal around the neck. The medal, sometimes found by collectors today, has the name and image of the cute baby doll on one side, a swastika cross on the other. The latter was an unfortunate choice. The swastika, an ancient good luck symbol, would become the hated Nazi emblem only four years later.

One reason for the dual marketing effort, it seems, was the expense of a nationwide campaign to launch the doll by radio, an advertising medium then in its infancy but growing fast. Children listening to the radio ads were urged to visit their local department store toy department to see the doll and pick up an entry blank for the "Win A Doll A Day" contest. Winners were announced later on the radio.

More than two decades later, in the 1950s, Horsman reused the familiar name for an all-new, all-vinyl Gold Medal Doll.

Gold Medal Baby: 18". Dressed in original outfit; note necklace medallion. $100.00. Courtesy Barbara Pio.

Gold Medal: In the early 1930s, Horsman sold a new version of Gold Medal Baby wearing this brass-colored medallion as a necklace. A few years later, the swastika, traditionally a good luck symbol, took on negative connotations after it was adopted as the Nazi emblem. $20.00. Courtesy Russ Sears, Chris Myer.

Gold Medal Baby: 17". All-composition infant, with original box and hang tag. $275.00. Courtesy Just Perfect Dolls & Antiques.

Gold Medal Baby: 19". Unplayed-with doll and box from the late 1930s. Probably a salesman's sample as it still has the stock number tag of the wholesale distributor, Butler Brothers. $300.00 Courtesy Sandra Tripp.

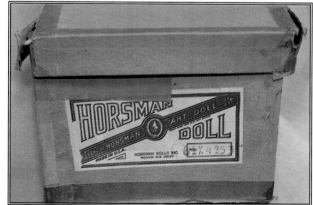

PETERKIN was another familiar name resurrected by Horsman. When the company lost the licensing rights to use the Campbell Kid image and name to American Character in 1928, it introduced a new Peterkin family of dolls that looked remarkably like the American Character Petite Campbell Kid lineup. A key distinction is that the point of the forelock of hair is centered on the Petite version but is combed to the left side of Peterkin's head.

After WWII, Horsman again regained exclusive license from the Campbell Soup Co. to make and market composition dolls with the familiar name and likeness. These new dolls were unveiled at the March 1947 Toy Fair in New York City.

"Old timers among the toy buying fraternity still speak frequently of the tremendous reception accorded that doll by the American public," an announcement in *Playthings* magazine noted. "Horsman Dolls, Inc., feels that the time is opportune to introduce this famous character to the new generation of American children."

And as expected, the updated and modernized version of the classic Campbell Kid doll was a success in the late 1940s, one of Horsman's last big hits of the composition era. The all-composition fully-jointed 12" boy and girl dolls had molded painted shoes and socks, molded brown hair, painted black eyes, and several different red and white outfits. For the boy, these included the famous chef's garb, romper shorts or overalls: for the girl, skirt or shorts.

Campbell Kid: 12". $350.00.

Campbell Kid: 12". All-composition Horsman Campbell Kid, circa 1948, in original outfit. Damaged hands. $200.00. Courtesy Gary Keller.

Campbell Kid: 12". In original outfit with Campbell Soup tag and box. $850.00. Courtesy Nancy Ringe.

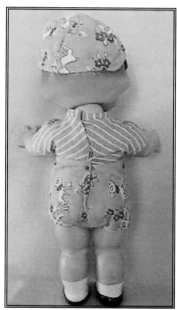

Campbell Kids: 12". $475.00 pair.
Courtesy McMasters Doll Auctions.

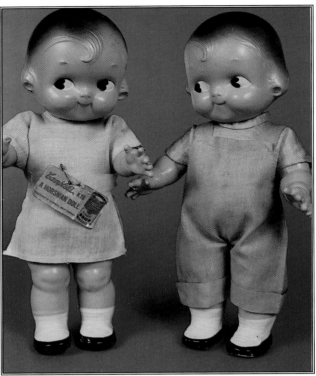

Campbell Kids: 12".
$275.00 pair. *Courtesy*
McMasters Doll Auctions.

Campbell Kids Twins: 12". $350.00 pair. *Courtesy McMasters*
Doll Auctions.

Campbell Kid: 12". $200.00.
Courtesy McMasters Doll Auctions.

Soup Chef: 12". Vintage 1948 Campbell Kid.
$475.00. Courtesy McMasters Doll Auctions.

Canadian Campbell Kid: 12". This is the Canadian version of the
1940s composition Campbell Kid, made under license by Dee and
Cee Doll Co. Note the thick painted eyelashes. $450.00. Courtesy Leslie
Falcon.

Rosebud: 24". Late 1940s doll with composition swivel head, shoulder plate, arms, and legs. $400.00. Courtesy Pat Lee.

Another of Horsman's recycled names was Rosebud, which first appeared in 1914 as **Baby Rosebud**, a Can't Break 'Em head, cloth body baby with bent legs. In 1928, a dimpled smiling **Dolly Rosebud**, now a sleep-eyed doll with mama crier, was sold as a big sister — in sizes from 17" to 22" — of Baby Dimples. By the mid-1930s, it was simply **Rosebud**, an updated toddler with mama crier, shiny glassene sleep eyes, mohair wig, and beautiful creamy complexion. And Rosebud appeared once more about 1950, as a soft vinyl doll that came in both white and black versions.

Other old familiar Horsman names found in the company's 1934 catalog include **Tynie Baby**, in four sizes, 13" to 20", and **Baby Dimples**, in sizes 15" to 27".

1930s Baby: 14½". Composition baby with mama crier, green tin sleep eyes. $150.00. Courtesy Valerie Zakzewski.

Baby Doll: 24". Chubby 1930s baby.
$75.00. Courtesy Tracey Baumgartner.

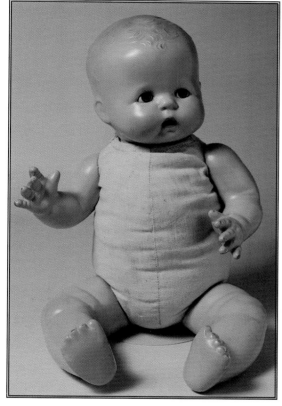

Curved Leg Baby: 16". From the 1930s.
$125.00.

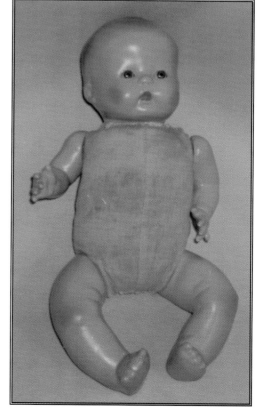

Curved Legs: 14". Marked H © C on back of neck;
possibly a Horsman doll. $80.00. Courtesy Dee Cermak.

Baby Doll: 21". Molded hair under strawberry blonde wig. $100.00. Courtesy Paula J. Giany.

Open Mouth Baby: 17". Molded hair baby has open mouth, red felt tongue. $250.00. Courtesy Diane Bucey Adolfson.

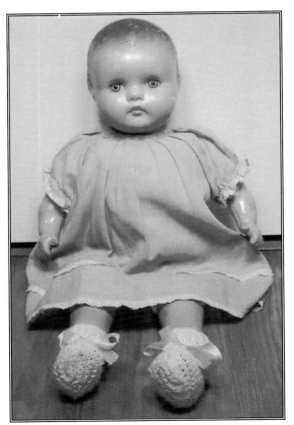

Mama Doll: 15". Doll with blue tin sleep eyes. $120.00. Courtesy Cindy Blach.

Rosebud: 24". All-original, all-composition doll.
$450.00. Courtesy Arlene Jensen.

Rosebud: 20". Early to mid-
1930s. $350.00.

Rosebud: 21". Rare black version from
1940s. $400.00.

Rosebud: 20". $325.00. Courtesy
McMasters Doll Auctions.

Sears Specials

In the 1930s and 1940s, various American doll manufacturers were contracted to make dolls for the major mail order firms, especially Sears, Roebuck & Co. For Sears, there were two important criteria, quality and value, and quite simply, value meant price.

Christmas catalogs of the era gave hints as to how the process worked.

"Twelve of the world's best doll manufacturers bid on these three big gorgeous dolls…but only two could make them to sell at this…price…. Only by ordering carloads early in the year…could we set such utterly low prices…. Sears bought thousands from Santa."

Often, it seems, it was Horsman that played Santa, coming in with the low bid to make carloads of dolls to Sears's specifications. Usually these dolls were sold under names that had been trademarked by the huge mail order firm. Sometimes the dolls themselves changed significantly from year to year, though the names were used Christmas after Christmas.

Composition Bride: 17". With blonde mohair wig, sleep eyes, and open mouth with teeth. $145.00.
Courtesy Tammy Nall.

Toddler: 18". $300.00. Courtesy McMasters Doll Auctions.

Pigtailed Girl: 15". $425.00. Courtesy McMasters Doll Auctions.

Candy Striper: 15". Horsman doll from mid-1940s, dressed as Candy Striper hospital aide. $350.00.

Bridegroom: 20". Groom in original black wool formal wear. $750.00. Courtesy Beverly Courtney, Carol Ferguson, House of Windsor Antiques.

Chubby and Baby Darling, shown in the 1938 Sears, Roebuck & Co. Christmas catalog are believed to have been made exclusively for Sears by Horsman.

In some cases, the catalog text noted that certain dolls were made by Horsman; the familiar name still connoted quality to most Americans. More often, though, there were few catalog clues as to the manufacturer. A study of Christmas catalogs of the 1930s and 1940s, however, suggests that the following Sears, Roebuck dolls were made by Horsman:

• Dolls named **Baby Sunshine, Miss Sunshine, Dorable, Dorable Baby, Dainty Dorothy, Dainty Baby, Baby Marie, Miss Marie, Little Miss Quality, Little Miss Dainty. Little Miss Gorgeous, Gorgeous, Glamour Girl, Grace, Joan, Our Beautiful Princess, Pinafore Darling, Pinafore Baby, Wonder Doll, Poppa-Momma,** and some of the **Happi-Time** dolls.

• Dolls with more generic names: **Turning Head Baby, Chubby, Chubby Baby, Coat Baby, Blanket Coat Baby, Real Cutie, Crying Baby,** and many more.

• Dolls described in catalog text as having Esmond cotton blanket cloth coats and hats; clothing of Duvetyn cotton or Celanese rayon; coats of simulated Persian lamb; marabou trimmed outfits; double-sprayed or waterproofed tinted enamel, washable composition; Poppa-Momma voices, and in post-World War II years, dolls made of Vinylite plastic.

Clues on tags, labels or boxes may help to identify Sears dolls made by Horsman.

The variety of Horsman-made Sears dolls during this period is amazing. They were mostly babies, but also toddlers and girl dolls. They came in all sizes, from 11" to 28", with heads of composition, hard rubber, and, in later years, plastics, with painted or sleep eyes with lashes, (including some with "rolling" or flirty eyes), with molded hair or wigs, mostly mohair but a few with human hair, with composition, rubber, vinyl or cloth bodies, stuffed with cotton or kapok, with criers or without.

Dual-voice dolls seem to have been popular starting in the late 1930s, with Ideal leading the way, but Horsman followed suit with its trademarked Poppa-Momma dolls, which cried for one parent or the other, depending on which direction they were tilted. These sorts of baby dolls appeared in Sears catalogs even into the 1950s.

To study the Sears catalogs on microfilm, available in many regional libraries in the U.S., is to see the history of American dolls unfolding.

Horsman made Baby Sunshine, 26", for Sears, Roebuck. The doll, dressed in Esmond blanket cloth coat and marabou-trimmed bonnet, was shown in the Sears 1939 Christmas catalog.

First to Say "Papa" and "Mama"

← $1.98

- Mama, Papa voice
- Sleeping eyes
- Coat and bonnet of Esmond blanket cloth
- Composition turning head—arms—legs

Now Daddy gets a break for this little darling says "Papa" as well as "Mama" depending on how you hold her. One of the sweetest, cuddliest babies we've seen—20 inches tall with soft cotton stuffed body, just the right size to hold in your arms. Her coat and bonnet are pink, genuine Esmond cotton blanket cloth. Bonnet is trimmed with rayon pile plush and tied with silk ribbon ties. Underneath she wears a white organdy dress—slip—and rubber panties. Rayon socks—bootees. Shpg. wt., 3 lbs.
49 V 3120—20-Inch "Papa"-"Mama" Doll $1.98

Dolls with a two-word vocabulary, "mama" and "papa" enjoyed a renewed popularity in the late 1930s. Sears began offering mama-papa dolls made by Horsman in its 1939 Christmas catalog. Unlike Ideal's Poppa-Mama doll which cried "mama" when tipped forward and "papa" when tilted back, this doll cried for her Mom when tipped to one side, and was Daddy's girl when tipped to the other.

Good Quality—Sears Sunshine Dolls

- ✓ Big Values for Thrifty Little Mothers
- ✓ Pretty, Natural Looking Sleeping Eyes
- ✓ Sunshine Dolls are Daintily Dressed
- ✓ Nicely Finished—Well Constructed

Baby Sunshine Finer Than Ever...Worth $3!

$1.98

- Lustrous glass-like eyes... long sweeping lashes.
- Big as a real baby...26 inches tall.
- Genuine Esmond blanket cloth coat and hat.
- Turns her pretty composition head...cries realistically.

Isn't she a lovely baby? She's the biggest bargain in Santa's 1940 pack! Her soft cotton-filled body is just the right size...she cuddles snugly up to her proud little mother. Pretty-as-a-picture composition head with sleeping glass-like eyes, sweeping lashes. Her rosebud mouth is slightly open to show teeny white teeth and a wee red tongue. Chubby arms, dimpled legs. Beautifully dressed in genuine cotton Esmond blanket cloth coat stitched with baby blue yarn and cunning Brownie-type peaked bonnet trimmed with fluffy marabou. Her dress is fine organdy with real lace edge. Dainty slip, rubber panties, cotton socks, bootees.
79 N 03175—Baby Sunshine. Shpg. wt., 4 lbs..............$1.98

So Sweet and Shy

$1.49

- A $2.00 value.
- Demure long-dress baby ...16 inches tall.
- Turning head...she can look most anywhere!
- Lifelike sleeping eyes with long sweeping lashes.
- Soft and cuddly, cotton filled body.
- Lovely organdy lace trimmed long dress.
- Dressy lace-trimmed ribbon-tied bonnet.

A fine quality long dress baby. So low priced it's almost too good to be true! And she's a real one. Your little girl will be so thrilled when she finds Baby Sunshine Christmas morning.

Her rosebud mouth looks so natural. Baby Sunshine's long dress is made of lovely organdy with satin like sheen ribbon rosettes . . . sweet little ribbon tied bonnet to match. Of course she wears rubber panties (all babies do), a long slip, rayon socks, and wee bootees. Shpg. wt., 2 lbs. 4 oz.
49 N 3114—Long Dress Baby...... $1.49

Sensational Value!

95c

- Features of regular $1.50 baby doll!
- Lifelike sleeping eyes ... long lashes.
- Open rosebud mouth; tiny teeth and red tongue.
- 16 inches tall. Waterproof composition head, arms and legs.
- Turning head. Smartly styled dress.
- Soft cotton filled body.

Any little mother would be proud to have this Baby Sunshine! Fun to hold because she's so cuddly. Turning composition head...she can look on either side. Inside tied arms, tied baby legs ...rosy dimpled knees. She cries too, just like a real baby. Dressed in a flaring-skirted organdy dress that makes a full circle when she sits! Dress is trimmed with val-type lace and shiny satin-like ribbon. Ruffled, ribbon-tied bonnet with net insert. Matching slip, rubber panties, rayon socks, tiny bootees. Shipping weight, 1 pound 12 oz.
49 N 3115—Dressed Baby.......... 95c

Baby Sunshine—Chest, Extra Outfit

$2.98

- Doll alone is worth $2.00!
- 18-inch soft cotton filled doll.
- Natural sleeping eyes, long lashes.
- Life-like turning composition head.
- 20x12½x7¾-inch wardrobe chest for Baby Sunshine, extra dress, bonnet.
- Pretty ruffled chest makes bed for doll.

Comes in organdy dress with Celanese rayon coat and ribbon-tied bonnet to match, slip, rubber panties, rayon socks, bootees. Extra dress, bonnet.
79 N 03599—Doll and Wardrobe. Shpg. wt., 6 lbs. 8 oz. $2.98

☒ PAGE 65 ..... DOLLS

Baby Sunshine, from the Sears 1940 catalog, came in 16", 18", and 26", the larger sizes wearing Esmond blanket cloth coat and hat.

Better Quality—Sears *Marie* Dolls

✔ Priced to Please Moderate Budgets
✔ Beautiful "Glass-Like" Sleeping Eyes
✔ Marie Dolls Wear Stylish Clothes
✔ Finer Dolls, Smaller Yet Prettier

CRIES POPPA-MOMMA

Now! *Baby Marie* Has Flirty Eyes, Too

$1.98 • Magic Rolling Glass-Like Eyes with Long Lashes. $2.98
49 N 3162 • Famous "Poppa-Momma" Voice. At Last Daddy Gets a Break ... this Lovable Baby Cries for Him, Too. • Turning Composition Head. 49 N 3161

The most talkative, the most talked-about doll of the year. Soft cotton filled body. Tongue, dainty white teeth, open rosebud mouth. Full cut, lace-trimmed organdy dress, ruffled bonnet with net insert; slip, rubber panties, rayon socks, bootees.

Glass-Like Eyes; Lashes | Rolling Glass-Like Eyes; Lashes
Shpg. wt. 1 lb. 1 oz. | Shipping weight, 3 lbs. 1 oz.
49 N 3160—14 in.....$1.98 | 49 N 3161—18 inches Tall.......$2.98

Nice Quality Clothes
• $3 Value Elsewhere.
• Sleeping glass-like eyes ... long lashes.
• Turning composition head ... rosebud mouth shows pretty lips—Beautiful features. $1.89
49 N 3162—Short Dress Baby ...$1.89

Rayon Taffeta Baby
• 18-in.—worth $3.
• Gleaming Celanese rayon coat, hat.
• Twinkling glass-like eyes—Lashes.
• Turning composition head... natural features. $1.98
49 N 3163—Shpg. wt., 3 lbs...$1.98

Big-as-Life 25-inch *Baby Marie*
• Has features of $4.00 doll.
• 25 in. tall ... right size to make a nice armful
• cuddly soft cotton-filled body.
• Turning composition head, arms, legs.
• Mischievous twinkle in her glass-like eyes ... but her long lashes are on demand She sleeps. She cries. $2.79
79 N 03164—Shipping weight, 4 pounds.........$2.79

SEARS LOVELY DOLLS ARE SOLD ON EASY TERMS ... See Page A, Center of Book.

PAGE 67 .... DOLLS

Baby Marie was part of a higher quality line of Horsman-made dolls in Sears' 1940 Christmas "Wish Book." The top of the line came with two-voice crier and flirty eyes.

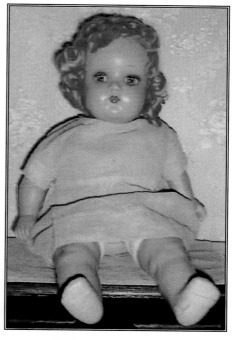

Baby Marie: 21". Sears doll has original cardboard and foil wrist tag. Made by Horsman exclusively for Sears, Roebuck & Co. $165.00. Courtesy Arlene Jensen.

Sears Doll: 16". Typical of medium-priced Horsman dolls sold by Sears during the 1940s. Mohair wig stapled to sides of composition head. $80.00.

Horsman's Bright Star line from the 1942 wholesale catalog of Butler Brothers. From left, pigtailed Betty, 15"; Honey, 18", and Judy, 21"; and, with ringlet wigs, Carol, 15"; Patty, 18", and Jean, 21".

Rosebud darlings from the 1942 Butler Brothers wholesale catalog. From left, Shirley, 21"; Doris, 23", and Julie, 25".

Dorable Baby, left, shown in the 1943 Sears catalog, came in 18" and 23" sizes. Momma-Poppa, right, was sold in 15" and 18" sizes.

1942 Chubby Gold Medal line as shown in Butler Brothers wholesale catalog. From left, Sue, 12"; Joan, 15"; Dottie, 17½", and Janet, 20".

"GOLD MEDAL" CHUBBY DOLLS

Sue Joan Dottie Janet

Enchanting Eyes: 20". Hard plastic doll with cloth body has "Enchanting Eyes," Horsman's term, circa 1950, for so-called flirty eyes that both open and close but also roll from side to side. $150.00.

Flirty Mama: 22". This mama doll has flirty eyes and long blonde mohair wig. Redressed. $50.00. Courtesy Ann Boregino.

Montgomery Ward's Dolls

Montgomery Ward, Sears's chief mail order competitor in the 1930s and 1940s, seems to have offered fewer types of dolls in its catalogs and relied less heavily on those made exclusively for the catalog retailer by manufacturers like Horsman.

A 1938 Montgomery Ward catalog headlined a "21-inch Horsman Doll//Blue Rayon Coat, Hat" for $1.98. "Easily worth $3," the text said of the cloth body girl doll with compo limbs and head, blue sleep eyes with long lashes, blonde mohair wig with long corkscrew curls.

But in the same catalog, 17" and 21" molded hair baby dolls, clearly made by Horsman, are identified by generic description only as "**Baby Doll** with Go-To-Sleep Eyes" and "**Our Finest Baby.**"

The 1943 Montgomery Ward Christmas catalog listed Horsman products as "Good quality, popular priced dolls." Pictured are A. 23" Baby with molded hair, two-voice crier and flirty eyes; B. 15" Baby with sleep eyes, mama crier, cotton-stuffed cloth body; C. 15" Doll with Braids, all-composition, sleep eyes, mohair wig with pigtails; D. 16" Doll in Organdy, all-composition, mohair ringlet wig, sleep eyes; E. 19½" Doll in Red Velveteen, all-composition, sleep eyes, real lashes.

More dolls from the 1943 Montgomery Ward holiday catalog. G. 20" Doll in Babushka, cloth body, composition head, arms, and legs, mohair ringlets, sleep eyes; H. 16½" Doll in Hooded Coat of beige brushed rayon, hood lined with red velveteen; J. 17" Toddler Doll, all-composition, sleep eyes, mohair ringlets, pink flannel coat and bonnet, trimmed with marabou; K. 19" Baby Doll Cries Mama and DaDa, soft cotton-stuffed body, compo head, arms, legs, with sleep eyes; L. 21" Baby Doll in Organdy, soft body stuffed with rayon and cotton fiber, composition legs, hands, and head with sleep eyes.

1944 Ward's catalog Horsman toddler and girl dolls. From left, 3. 17" Toddler, all-composition with molded hair, sleep eyes, 4. 14" Toddler, all-composition; 10. 14" undressed Chubby Doll. Catalog text says "It is fun to make clothes for this cunning Horsman doll." 11. 15" undressed girl doll with mohair ringlet wig, came with shoes, but it was left to the little girl or her Mom to "make and fit your own doll clothes."

1944 Ward's Christmas catalog dolls. Lower row, from left, 7. 19" baby Doll in Organdy, with molded hair and sleep eyes, 8. 15" Baby Doll, soft cotton-stuffed body, compo head, arms, and legs, sleep eyes, 9. 21" Poppa-Momma Baby with two-voice crier, molded hair. Upper row, from left, 10. 22" Premium Baby Doll, with mama crier, flirty eyes, molded hair, bent-leg composition baby legs, 11. 21" Baby Doll in Pinafore, with mohair ringlet wig, glassene sleep eyes.

1944 Ward's Black Dolls: "Of well-known Horsman quality" these are "dainty, lovable Colored Baby dolls," the Christmas catalog noted. All are "exquisitely tinted a warm brown with sparkling brown glassene sleeping eyes." Lower row, from left, 1. 20" Colored Baby, composition head with molded hair, soft cotton-stuffed body. 2. 17" Baby in Pinafore, with black mohair ringlets, flock-dot cotton dress and bonnet. 3. 20" Colored Baby with black mohair curls. Top row, from left, 4. 16" Colored Baby, molded hair, white organdy dress and bonnet. 5. 23" Colored Baby with black mohair wig, white organdy dress and bonnet. At $6.98, this was the most expensive doll on the page. 6. 18" Colored Baby has molded hair, pink rayon coat, net trimmed cape collar and matching bonnet, white flock-dot cotton dress.

In the 1943 Ward's Christmas Book, a 19" baby that "cries Ma-Ma and Da-Da," was described as having hair molded and painted, glassene sleeping eyes with real lashes, and an embroidered, white organdy dress and matching bonnet with double net ruffle, white slip, and pink knitted panties. The text specifically noted it was "A Horsman doll."

The catalog clearly indicates three levels of dolls, ranked by quality and price, that Montgomery Ward sold that year. Effanbee's well-known "name" dolls, including Little Lady, Skippy soldier and sailor, Sweetie Pie, Brother and Sister are shown in full color and called "the best made dolls in the world." The Horsman-made babies and girls are labeled "good quality, popular priced dolls." The third tier, unidentified as to maker and distinctly cut-rate merchandise, is called simply, "low priced dolls…almost unbreakable."

The 1944 Christmas Book features a two-page spread displaying a group of wonderful Horsman baby dolls, apparently representing an upgrade in quality and price from the previous holiday season. What is especially interesting is that six of the 11 dolls were black babies.

The catalog text notes that Ward offered them "in response to many requests for well-made, well-designed colored dolls…of well known Horsman quality. They are exquisitely tinted a warm brown, with sparkling brown glassene sleeping eyes, real lashes. Lips are shaded a delicate rose… Dainty baby clothing is carefully made and finished."

These "colored baby dolls" except for their slightly darker complexion, looked nearly identical to the five white baby dolls shown on the facing page. They came in sizes from 16" to 23" and were priced from $3.49 to $6.95, significantly more than the so-called "popular value" range.

Ward catalogs also are useful for identifying and studying Horsman dolls from these two decades, however, unlike the microfilmed Sears catalog collection, they are difficult to find, even in major U.S. libraries. However, Montgomery Ward donated its complete catalog archives from 1874 to 1985, when it ended mail order sales, to the library of the University of Wyoming's American Heritage Center at Laramie, Wyoming, where they are available to doll researchers. The same collection includes later catalogs of Ward mail order competitors, Aldens (1958 – 1981), J.C. Penney (1963 – 1982), and Spiegel (1962 – 1983), as well as Sears, Roebuck.

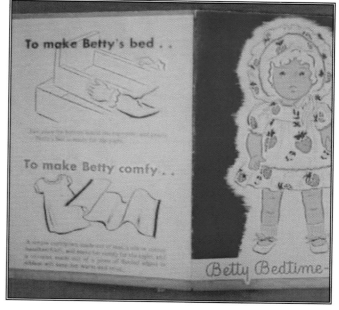

Betty Bedtime: 18". 1940s all-original marked Horsman doll with cloth body, composition head, lower arms, and legs, came with instruction booklet for converting her box, marked Betty Bedtime, into a ruffled bed. Neither box nor instruction booklet mentioned Horsman. May have been sold through one of the mail order catalog houses. $300.00. Courtesy Stephanie Kornreich.

"Back again" after the war was the Sears "Wonder Doll," left, in 17½" and 19½" sizes, shown in the 1947 Christmas "Wish Book." Other dolls were A. 15" Crying Baby, with long 17" dress of fine cotton with embroidery and lace trim. B. 16½" Lovable Crying Baby, with lifelike rubber skin arms and legs that "feel like a real baby's," cloth body and composition head. C. 16½" Chubby Toddler, all-composition doll with sleep eyes, print cotton dress and bonnet.

The Class of 1937

Perhaps the most innovative of Horsman's 1930s dolls were the **Whatsit** pair, **Roberta** and **Naughty Sue**. "Whatsit Dolls are truly different!" read a promotional announcement in the May 1937 issue of the trade publication *Toys and Bicycles*. "There are two distinct models, each with a different facial expression. They are produced under a special license and will be featured in *The Whatsit*, a newspaper for boys and girls, with a circulation of over three million copies. Further promotional efforts by The Whatsit licensor will consist of an extensive nationwide publicity campaign by radio, newspaper and other media."

This independent publication for youngsters had bigger plans. It announced a "Design Club" with art contests. Youthful winners' drawings were to be published as Whatsit stamps to be sent to subscribers. Special albums to hold 96 different stamps also were offered free to children who wrote to the newspaper's Park Avenue address in New York City.

1937 Regal advertisement introducing the whimsical Whatsit dolls.

The Whatsit newspaper for boys and girls licensed Horsman to make Whatsit dolls.

Girl: 13". Horsman doll from late 1930s with mohair wig in pigtails. $200.00. Courtesy Bev Mitchell.

The Whatsit is virtually unremembered today. But one vintage copy found recently indicates that in 1938 it was being distributed free to children through Safeway grocery stores. It's doubtful, however, that it was as successful as Horsman had hoped when it entered into the licensing agreement with the publisher.

The all-composition Whatsit dolls came in 14" and 16" sizes. They had cute character faces, and their right arm was bent like Effanbee's Patsy. The dolls came dressed in cotton print outfits and laced leatherette shoes. Each was marked with her name and © 1937 Horsman. Cardboard wrist tags identified them as Whatsit Dolls// by children// for children// A Genuine Horsman Doll.

Roberta had brown sleep eyes and her brown painted hair was molded with a part in the middle and braids curled into buns over her ears. Her mouth was closed and puckered. Naughty Sue also had brown hair, but it was molded into a topknot, tied with a big hair ribbon. Her eyes were painted, big, blue, and side glancing. Her mouth was open-closed, and her molded tongue was visible, attesting to her naughtiness.

Naughty Sue: 14". Whatsit doll with molded topknot where hair-bow was tied. $400.00.

Roberta: 14". Whatsit doll with molded hair curled into buns over her ears. $400.00.

Similar and perhaps a later addition to the Whatsit series was **Jeanie**, also in 14" and 16" sizes, but with a cloth body, mama crier, and swing legs. Her composition character head had a similar quizzical expression with small pursed lips and brown celluloid-over-tin sleep eyes without lashes. Jeanie's molded brown-painted hair had a slight topknot and bangs. Also released in 1937, she was marked Jeanie// Horsman.

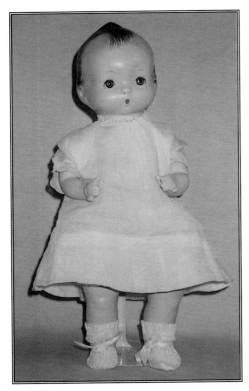

Jeanie: 14". Original teddy, dress, and socks. $300.00. Courtesy Dee Cermak.

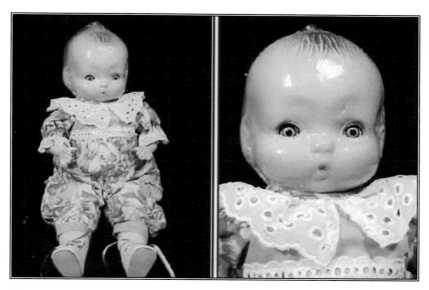

Jeanie: 14". One of Horsman's new dolls in 1937. Re-dressed. $150.00.
Courtesy Flo Burnside.

SISTER, introduced by Horsman in the same year, was very similar in facial and body characteristics, but, at 23" tall, was substantially larger. She had the same slight top knot and celluloid/tin sleep eyes. She was marked Sister// © 1937 Horsman. Brother, her 21" companion, had big brown sleep eyes and tiny mouth, but an expression somewhat less cartoon-like than Sister and the Whatsit types. He was marked Brother// © 1937 Horsman.

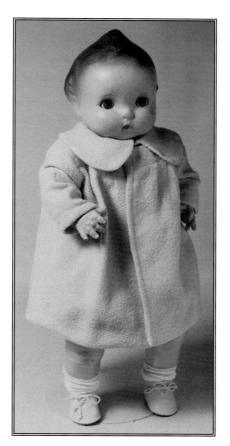

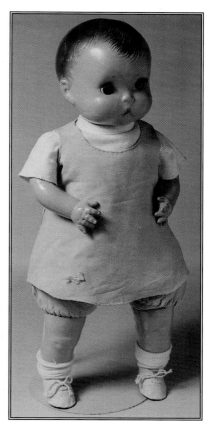

Sister: 23". Whimsical composition face, cloth body and upper legs. $350.00.

Brother: 21". Marked Brother // 1937 Horsman. $350.00.

Seemingly related to Jeanie was **Buster**, a little-known and rarely found doll today. He is known to have been made in a 20" size with a soft, one-piece terrycloth body, apparently intended as an infant's doll. He was marked on the back of his composition head, Buster // C. 1937 Horsman.

Another result of Horsman's 1937 burst of inspiration was 12" **Jo-Jo**, a more traditional character doll, owing more in looks to Patsy than to the Whatsits, and therefore, probably, more successful, since many more Jo-Jos are found today than Whatsit dolls.

Jo-Jo was an all-composition toddler and came in boy and girl models. These differed in dress, of course, and the fact that the girl version had a blonde or brown mohair wig with pigtails over the doll's molded hair. Jo-Jo had a closed mouth and either painted blue eyes or blue tin sleep eyes. The doll was marked Jo-Jo// © 1937 Horsman.

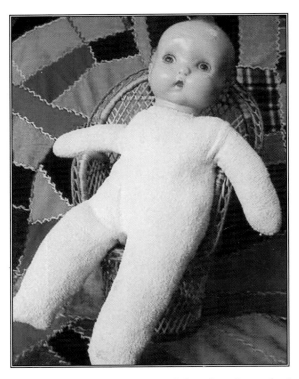

Buster: 20". Rare composition head marked Buster // C. 1937 Horsman, on a soft-stuffed terrycloth one-piece body. $80.00. Courtesy Linda Woodhouse, Frances Margulieux.

Jo-Jo: 12". Three toddlers. $250.00 each. Courtesy Gay Smedes.

Jo-Jo: 12". All-composition with pigtailed wig over molded hair. $150.00. Courtesy Marseille Bunk.

Jo-Jo: 12". $350.00. Courtesy McMasters Doll Auctions.

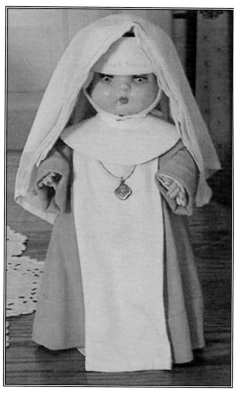

Jo-Jo: 12". In the 1930s, this doll was lovingly redressed in great detail as a nun, possibly from the order of the Sister Servants of the Holy Ghost of Perpetual Adoration, the so-called Pink Nuns. "Spiritui Sancto" is embroidered in script on the bonnet. $300.00. Courtesy Karen Scheel.

Jo-Jo: 12". Composition toddler in original dress, with matching panties and bonnet. $300.00. Courtesy Bernice Allen.

Jo-Jo: 12". Vintage dress but without shoes and socks. $75.00. Courtesy The Doll Broker, Rebecca Branscome.

After the War

Some manufacturers halted doll production in the latter years of World War II because of critical shortages of mohair and metals. Thanks to Sears, Roebuck catalogs, we know that Horsman somehow continued to manufacture some dolls throughout the war. We can assume, though, that the company, like many toy makers, also turned to production of items totally unrelated to dolls. Just what these products were we do not know, but we can surmise that they were made of brand new plastic materials. It is known that by 1944, Horsman engineers and technicians already were familiar with plastics. Shortly after the war ended, the company was ready, several years before other doll manufacturers, to produce plastic dolls.

It was a time of experimentation. Early plastic dolls from the post-war years tend to suffer a number of problems today, including fading, discoloration, and stickiness caused by the leaching of the plasticizer or softening agent from the vinyl. While not exempt from such problems, Horsman dolls of the era seem to have fared significantly better over time, probably because of the plastics know-how gained by Horsman during the war.

Horsman ads in the trade publications indicate the company was struggling to catch up to a built-up demand. We "hope that in 1946 it will be possible to satisfy your needs for America's best known and best loved dolls," one advertisement said. Initially, it seems, the company simply began turning out increasing numbers of the composition-and-cloth baby dolls it sold during the war.

Plastic Baby: 22". Circa 1950, marked Horsman baby with hard plastic head with molded hair beneath the mohair wig. Soft vinyl skin body is beginning to darken. $75.00. Courtesy Joyce MacWilliamson.

Transitional Baby: 18". From the late 1940s, this Horsman baby has a composition head with strawberry blonde mohair wig, a cloth body with mama crier, and soft vinyl arms and legs. $125.00. Courtesy Jeanne Swafford.

In 1946, the first of its **Fairy Skin** dolls quietly appeared on the toy market. Trade advertising did not begin to mention these sorts of dolls until early the following year, at first referring to them simply as "new and sensational 'SKIN-TYPE BABY DOLLS.'" These dolls had a soft stuffed skin of thin vinyl and an unjointed one-piece body and limbs. Heads usually were made of a soft molded vinyl, which Horsman would later refer to as Vinylite. Some Fairy Skin babies had hard plastic or even composition heads, like 20" **Chubby Ruthie** from the very late 1940s.

During the next several years, other Horsman dolls were similarly made with a skin of natural rubber, rather than vinyl plastic. These the company referred to as **Latex Skin** dolls.

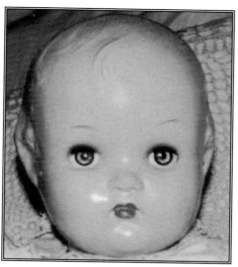

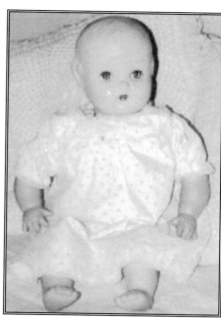

Green-Eyed Mama: 21". From the 1940s, this marked Horsman doll has composition head and soft-stuffed latex skin arms and legs. $75.00. Courtesy Danielle Brumit.

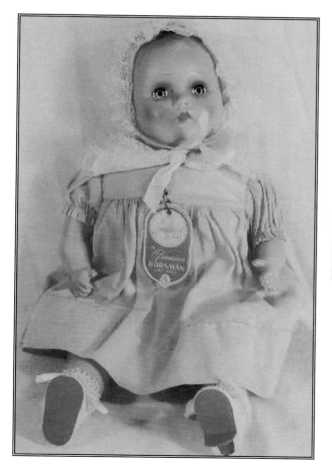

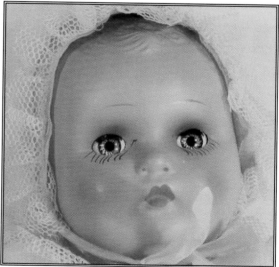

Baby Doll: 14". Composition head doll from the late 1940s, with original lace-trimmed pink bonnet and dress, box, and hang tag identifying her as a Horsman Art Doll. $200.00.

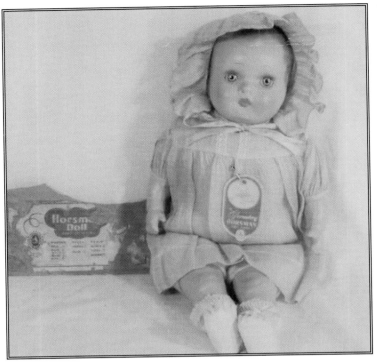

Composition Baby: 15″. Doll from about 1948, with Horsman-marked box and cardboard hang tag. $200.00.

Baby: 21″. $275.00. Courtesy McMasters Doll Auctions.

Horsman advertising in 1947 referred also to the "new Baby Dolls with 'skin-like' arms and legs." These babies had traditional cloth bodies and heads of either molded Vinylite plastic or traditional composition.

Bi-Bye Baby had vinyl hands and head, with painted eyes. Its cloth body was made like a mitt into which a child could put her hand to use the doll like a puppet. The 12″ doll looked like a newborn with wide open mouth, lustily crying. She was dressed in soft flannel baby clothes and came wrapped in a patterned — the doll's name printed repeatedly — pink and white baby blanket. Bi-Bye Baby was marked Horsman on the back of the head.

By late 1947, Horsman was selling a series of dolls it called **Softee**, all or in part made of soft molded Vinylite plastic. In the April 1948 issue of *Playthings* magazine, it advertised them as "soft, nearest human in looks and feel;

retains the accurate detail of the original sculpture; arms and legs washable with soap and water. Immune to scuffing, peeling, cracking. Will not rot or mildew. An entirely new doll in material and technique."

Snuggle Softee was called the "perfect crib companion!" The soft, cuddly doll, safe even for an infant, had head and hands of molded Vinylite, with body and legs of stuffed cloth. In 1950, it appears in the Horsman catalog with a "squalling" open mouth with tongue.

A doll with a similar open-closed crying mouth and molded tongue, commonly called **Squalling Baby,** came in several sizes, 14″, 18″ and 20″, and is marked Lastic Plastic 49. Although often attributed to Horsman, that connection has not been confirmed through advertising or catalog listing.

Also in 1948, Horsman reintroduced its 1930s drinking-wetting doll Buttercup, with its former rubber body and legs now made of soft Vinylite. It was called **Softee Buttercup**.

In 1949, **Cry Baby** was introduced as a "sensational new Softee doll" with special key-wind mechanism. "Lay her down and she cries. Pick her up and she stops crying," the advertising text explained. A 21" composition head mama doll with cloth body and Fairy Skin type arms and legs had the same sort of key-wind crier device.

Cry Baby: 24". Transitional doll from circa 1949, composition head, cloth body, and vinyl limbs, with a key-wind mechanism. The doll moves and cries when laid down. $175.00. Courtesy Deborah Miller.

Cry Baby: 23". Closed mouth version with composition head, cloth body, and vinyl limbs, from the late 1940s. Wind-up cry mechanism not working. $130.00. Courtesy Mary Loy.

Baby: 12". Late 1940s Horsman baby with closed mouth and molded hair, all-original with tag and box. $250.00. Courtesy Stephanie Kornreich.

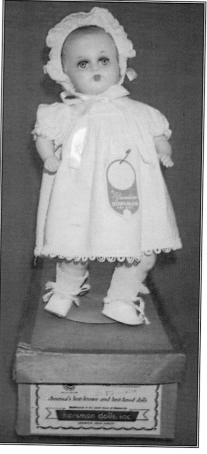

Attractive straight-legged girl and mama dolls, with either composition or hard plastic heads, are seen in Horsman advertising from 1947, continuing the limited line product policy the company had followed since the 1930s. Invariably, these were attractive, good quality dolls, well-dressed in lovely outfits, but at what the ads called "reasonable prices."

In 1950, the company celebrated its 85th birthday. Its catalog included several new dolls with familiar old names: **Tynie Baby**, a newborn with a soft plastic head, arms, and legs, and **Gold Medal**, a straight-legged standing doll with arms, legs, and bodies of soft-stuffed natural latex rubber.

At the midpoint of the twentieth century, there still were a few Horsman composition dolls. Still listed in the catalog were the composition **Campbell Kids**, which had been reintroduced three years earlier, and **Bright Star**, although *Playthings* magazine noted that all-plastic Bright Stars "in refreshing new styles" also were available.

But the era that E. I. Horsman Co., Inc. had kicked off a half-century earlier with its Billiken was quickly winding down. By 1951, the last composition doll had disappeared from the Horsman catalog.

The company, however, would turn out many wonderful vinyl dolls in the years ahead.

Hard Plastic Girl: 17". All-plastic doll marked Horsman. Open-closed mouth with four teeth, red mohair wig, wearing original blue dress with full skirt and bodice with lace inserts and tiny buttons. $185.00. Courtesy Shawn Stevens, Sister Act Two.

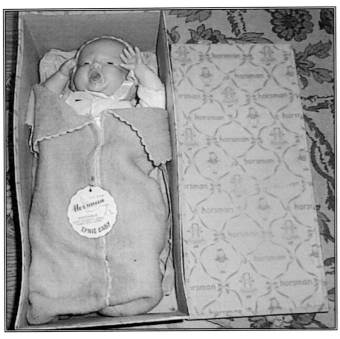

Tynie Baby: 21". The 1950 catalog introduced this pliable plastic Vinylite infant as "the newest member of the vast Horsman family." $75.00.

Hard Plastic: 16". Late-1940s girl made of hard Butyrate plastic, with original mohair wig with brass hair clips. Redressed in vintage outfit. $100.00. Courtesy Diane Chappell.

Hard Plastic: 15½". Painted hard plastic, dark-colored plastic visible on fingers where paint has rubbed off. Marked Horsman on back of neck. Dressed in pink flocked gown with attached muslin slip, matching headpiece stapled to head over mohair wig. Silver center snap sandals. May be costumed as Cinderella. $150.00. Courtesy Mary Whitney.

Glamour Girl: 19". All hard plastic doll marked Horsman on back of neck. Wearing bra, garters, and panty with sewn pink flower decoration under satin robe that opens in front to expose rouged knees. $400.00.

Bright Star: 17". 1940s all-original doll. $200.00.
Courtesy Joan Nickel.

Bright Star: 15". Circa 1950, all hard plastic doll with green sleep eyes, eye shadow, open mouth with felt tongue. $125.00. Courtesy Kathy DeFinis.

Bright Star Bride: 15". All hard plastic doll with paper hang tag, from the late 1940s. Original bridal costume with veil, gown with delicate lace trim, slip, panties, shoes and socks, holding bouquet of fabric flowers, netting, and ribbon. $250.00. Courtesy Kandy Ferriby.

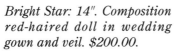

Bright Star: 14". Composition red-haired doll in wedding gown and veil. $200.00.

Shadow Wave: 18½". Horsman introduced Saran wigs in 1951, making it possible to wash and curl a doll's hair. Shadow Wave was its answer to Ideal's Toni home permanent doll. $175.00. Courtesy Gay Baron.

Epilogue

In the 1950s, 1,000 to 1,200 full- and part-time employees at the Trenton factory turned out as many as 1.5 million quality dolls a year. The large, skilled, and stable workforce was one of the company's greatest assets, but it was expensive. The unionized workers were earning substantially more than their counterparts in New York City doll factories.

After Horsman Dolls, Inc. threatened to close down in 1952, the union made wage concessions that kept the plant operating for eight more years. But by 1960, labor costs again had become a serious problem, and Horsman did close the Trenton factory, moving to a new, spacious, non-union facility in South Carolina.

For much of the next quarter-century, Horsman would enjoy a resurgence of profitability, employing more than 600 workers who turned out millions of high quality vinyl dolls in hundreds of different styles.

For well over two decades, beginning in the 1960s, the creative guiding light for Horsman's dolls was Irene Szor, who came to the company from competitor Sayco. She was the company's principal designer into the early 1980s when she left for a time, only to return shortly as the vice president of research and development.

By the 1980s, however, virtually all U.S. doll manufacturing had ended, with production shifted to the Orient with its cheaper labor costs. Horsman remained one of the last and the largest American doll company still manufacturing in the United States. Stubbornly, the company resisted extensive TV advertising and refused to shift its production from South Carolina to overseas sources.

Horsman stuck to its longtime formula, manufacturing a limited range of moderately priced basic but well-made children's dolls. Horsman did not change, but unfortunately, the toy market did. Children were asking for the mass-marketed dolls they saw in the TV commercials.

Horsman Dolls, Inc., which had gone through several changes in ownership, saw its sales, production, and workforce shrink. Eventually, in 1986, it laid off its remaining 150 employees and closed the factory at Cayce, South Carolina.

Drew Industries, its corporate parent, sold what remained of Horsman — mostly its venerable name — to a company called Gata Box, Ltd. On a modest scale, the new owner began selling dolls manufactured in Hong Kong. Gata's products were directed toward both children and adult doll collectors, a specialized market that grew rapidly during the 1980s.

In 1985, its last year of U.S. production, Horsman Dolls, Inc., gambled that doll collectors would buy modern vinyl reproductions of well-known and well-loved composition doll favorites. That year, the company brought out a replica of a Horsman 1928 baby doll. Not only did buyers take to it, the reproduction won the prestigious Doll of the Year Award for 1985.

Gata Box built upon this success after acquiring the Horsman name, producing limited editions of other classic dolls from the past. Tynie Baby Twins, copies of Horsman's 1924 favorite, were issued in 1986. In subsequent years, other reproduction editions followed, each limited to 2,000 to 3,000 dolls: HEbee and SHEbee in 1987; Billiken and Ella Cinders in 1988; Sister and Bright Star Baby in 1989; Dimples in 1990; Brother in 1991; Buttercup in 1992; Baby Rosebud in 1993, and Pinafore Baby in 1996. Horsman's 130th anniversary in 1995 was marked by a special reproduction of Baby Dimples.

In October 1999, Gata Box Ltd. went out of business, succeeded by a new corporation known as Horsman, Ltd., headquartered in Great Neck, Long Island, NY. Millennium Edition dolls, including a pair of small Campbell Kids dressed as a bride and groom, were sold in 2000 and 2001. Horsman, Ltd. continues to market dolls made in China, according to Barbara Kaufman, a company spokesperson.

1960 Horsman catalog.

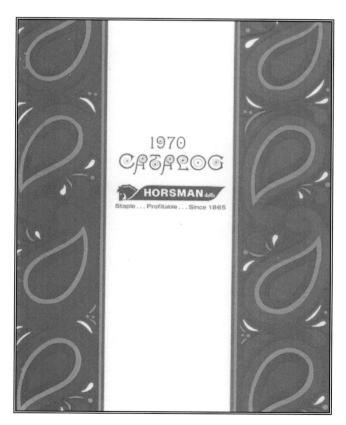

1970 Horsman catalog.

1980 Horsman catalog.

1990 Horsman catalog.

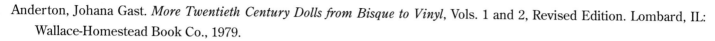

Books

Anderton, Johana Gast. *More Twentieth Century Dolls from Bisque to Vinyl*, Vols. 1 and 2, Revised Edition. Lombard, IL: Wallace-Homestead Book Co., 1979.

——————. *The Collector's Encyclopedia of Cloth Dolls*. Wallace-Homestead, 1984.

——————. *Twentieth Century Dolls from Bisque to Vinyl*. Wallace-Homestead, 1971.

Casanova, Grace Hegger. *With Love from Gracie: Sinclair Lewis*, 1912 – 1925. New York City, NY: Harcourt, Brace & Co., 1951.

Coleman, Dorothy S., Elizabeth A. Coleman, and Evelyn J. Coleman. *The Collector's Encyclopedia of Dolls,* Vols. 1 and 2. New York, NY: Crown Publishers Inc., 1968 and 1986.

Edward, Linda. *Cloth Dolls from Ancient to Modern*. Atglen, PA: Schiffer Publishing Ltd., 1997.

Falk, Byron A., Jr., and Valerie R. Falk. *Personal Name Index to the New York Times Index, 1851 – 1974*. Succasunna, NJ: Roxbury Data Interface.

Foulke, Jan. *Blue Book of Dolls and Values*, 1st Edition (with Thelma Bateman), 2nd – 14th Editions. Cumberland and Grantsville, MD: Hobby House Press, 1974 – 1999.

Gibbs, Patikii. *Horsman Dolls, 1950 – 1970*. Paducah, KY: Collector Books, 1985.

Husfloen, Kyle D. (ed.). *Book of Collectible Dolls*. Dubuque, IA: The Babka Publishing Co., 1976.

Jackman, Rilla Evelyn. *American Arts*. Chicago, IL: Rand McNally & Co., 1928.

Judd, Polly, and Pam Judd. *Composition Dolls, Identification and Price Guide,* Vols. 1 (1928 – 1955) and 2 (1909 – 1928). Hobby House Press, 1991 and 1994.

——————. *Hard Plastic Dolls, Identification and Price Guide,* Vols. 1 and 2. Hobby House Press, 1985 and 1989.

Moyer, Patsy. *Doll Values, Antique to Modern,* 1st – 4th Editions. Collector Books, 1997 – 2000.

——————. *Modern Collector Dolls,* 1st-4th Series. Collector Books, 1997 – 2000.

Smith, Patricia R. *Doll Values, Antique to Modern,* 1st – 12th Editions. Collector Books, 1979 – 1996.

——————. *Modern Collector Dolls*, 1st – 8th Series. Paducah, KY: Collector Books, 1973 – 1996.

Van Patten, Joan F., and Linda Lau. *Nippon Dolls & Playthings: Identification and Values*. Paducah, KY: Collector Books, 2001.

Periodicals and Catalogs

Bangor Daily News, Bangor, ME, 1979

Doll News, 1976 – 2000 (United Federation of Doll Clubs)

Doll Reader, 1976 – 2000 (Cumberland Publishing Inc.)

E.I. Horsman catalogs, 1893, 1912, 1914, 1915, 1932, 1950

Lakeview Journal, Lakeview, CT, 1962, 1970

Montgomery Ward catalogs, 1930 – 1950

New York Times, 1890 – 2000

Playthings, 1910 – 1950 (McCready Publishing Co. and successors)

Port Washington News, newspaper, Port Washington, NY, 1914

Sears, Roebuck & Co. catalogs, 1930 – 1950

The American Stationer, 1890

The State, Columbia, SC, 1986 – 1990

Toys & Novelties, 1910 – 1950

Trenton Times, Trenton, NJ, 1950 – 1960

Articles

"A Maker of Dolls." *The Bulletin* (Women's Club of Upper Montclair, NJ), April 1926, pg. 1.

"Back from Europe," *Playthings*, June 1910, pg. 186.

"Dolls – Made in America." *Fortune*, December 1936, pg. 103.

"Edward Imeson Horsman." *The National Cyclopedia of American Biography*, Vol. 3, pg. 274.

"E.I. Horsman, Father of the Doll Industry." Elizabeth A. Coleman, *The Antique Journal,* January 1963, pg. 21.

"E.I. Horsman's Golden Anniversary." *Playthings*, January 1915, pg. 148.

"Guise and Dolls: The Rise of the Doll Industry and the Gender of Material Culture, 1830 – 1930." Miriam Formanek-Brunell, PhD. (Doctoral dissertation, 1990).

"If All Doll Babies Don't Look Alike…." *New York Evening Sun*, December 16, 1918.

"Journals. 1898, 1901" Edward I. Horsman Jr. (Unpublished, courtesy John Arbeeny).

"Making the Character Doll." *Playthings*, June, 1912, pg. 9.

"Pioneers in the Toy Trade, Edward Imeson Horsman." *Playthings*, January 1908.

"Prepares Grandest Meals with not a Thing to Eat." E.A. Teall. *Newark* (NJ) *Evening News*, February 18, 1936.

"Sisters of Santa Claus." Lillian Jeffreys Petri. *New York Herald*, December 6, 1914.

"Stories for Liz." Helen Fox Trowbridge, *Family Annals*, June 1958, (Unpublished, courtesy Helen Hoffman)

"The Death of E. I. Horsman." *Playthings*, August 1918.

"Toyman of Toytown." *McClure's*, November, 1913, pgs. 191 – 196.

"Toyman at Play." *Playthings*, August 1917.

About the Author

Don Jensen and his wife Arlene began collecting dolls nearly 20 years ago when his mother gave them her treasured childhood antique bisque doll. They soon focused on American-made composition dolls from the first half of the twentieth century and found collecting them was a hobby they could truly enjoy together.

He is a retired newspaperman with 34 years experience as a daily newspaper writer and editor. A freelance writer as well, he has written for national magazines on various subjects since 1967. Don has been a frequent contributor to *Doll Reader, Doll News, Contemporary Doll Collector,* and other doll magazines. He has edited doll collectors' reference books, and for two years he and his wife served as associate editors for *Doll News,* for which they received the United Federation of Doll Clubs' 1998 Award of Merit for contributions to that magazine.

He is a local historian, winner of state awards, and national nominations for writings — books, magazine and newspaper articles — on local history subjects. He is an experienced doll history researcher and an expert on composition dolls and was selected as a member of the honorary International Doll Academy. Don has presented seminars and programs and has served as judge in UFDC national convention and regional conference competitions.

He and Arlene — and their many composition dolls — live in southern Wisconsin.

Don Jensen.

Index

Index

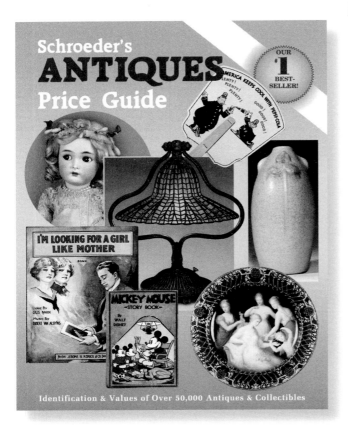